Melissa's Hat Trick

Melissa Meshishnek

ISBN-13:978-0692753972

Cover Photo by Michelle Davies

DEDICATION

In loving memory of my brother

Michael James McCready

October 1949-October 1969

And to my husband, my forever man, Michael

Hat trick: *noun* – chiefly in ice hockey or soccer, the scoring of three goals in a game by one player.

ACKNOWLEDGMENTS

In July 1987 my husband Michael vowed to love me "in sickness and in health." Twenty-five years later, that vow was sorely tested. It all began with a breast cancer diagnosis. After surgery, chemotherapy, and radiation therapy, I triumphed over that vicious disease. But seven months after my last radiation treatment, I was diagnosed with papillary thyroid cancer. One month after completing all the thyroid cancer therapies, I was diagnosed with lentiginous junctional nevus, a form of skin cancer.

Throughout my battles with cancer and the myriad debilitating side effects and illnesses that followed, Michael was a superior caregiver. He was the lifejacket that kept me afloat during the times my diseases threatened to take me under. His support manifested itself in many different ways; it was the singular constant, positive thing throughout my hellish journey. It's been ten years since my initial cancer diagnosis, and I'm still fighting to reclaim my health. Michael's support and enduring love has never wavered. I thank God every single day for my husband.

To my superb team of physicians:

Dr. Lincoln Snyder (my breast surgeon)- God is glorified in your work. I have no doubt that He led me to you. Keep those prayer cards in your reception area; seeing them was a miracle to me, and will be to others.

Dr. Tenley Lawton (my plastic surgeon)- I know it was a big job; bless you for taking it on when others would not.

Dr. Greg Angstreich (my oncologist)- You really *do* set the standard for excellence in your field. Chemotherapy was the scariest thing I've ever experienced, but your expertise and superior knowledge of oncological medicine reassured me that I was in the very best hands. Thank you for treating me with compassion and concern, for listening to me with your heart as well as your ears, and for never minimizing my fears. Thank you for being patient with Michael and graciously answering his never ending pharmacological questions!

Dr. Thomas Simko (my radiologist)- Thank you for making my radiation treatments a walk in the park. I was blessed to have found another outstanding physician with a stellar staff.

Dr. Kristin Egan (my ENT)- Thank you for getting that damned thyroid cancer out, and for leaving such a tiny scar. Your beautiful work even amazes other physicians!

Dr. Joseph C. Lee (my psychiatrist)- Long before my cancer diagnosis, you set me on the path to "mental healthiness." What you taught me proved to be an invaluable asset; I was able to maintain my sanity (pretty much) by using the tools I had learned over my years in therapy with you.

Dr. Robert Fenton (my orthopedic surgeon)- you were my first favorite doctor so many years ago; you fixed my back, my foot, my hand—and that was *before* the cancers struck! Now that my life has become a never-ending battle with long-term side effects from chemo and radiation, I am still able to turn to you to patch me back together again. God Bless you.

Emad Michael (my pharmacist)- You were always one step ahead of the game, ensuring that whatever medication I needed was ready and waiting for me. You and your staff continue to treat me like a family member, not a customer. This tiny little suburb of El Segundo is so blessed to have such a superior pharmacist.

And to Michelle Davies- a photographer who offered to take my picture for the book cover. Although we had never met, Michelle drove from Ventura to El Segundo for a photo shoot, took about fifty pictures, assisted in preparing a book cover, and then refused to be reimbursed for any of her services. She told me she just wanted to be a part of my project; in return for her services, she requested only an autographed copy of this book. I am forever grateful for your amazing generosity, Michelle.

PART ONE

Forewarned, Forearmed

PART TWO

King Me

Melissa Meshishnek

Part One

Forewarned, forearmed; to be prepared is half the victory

Miguel de Cervantes

Melissa Meshishnek

THE MANGLER

Moral of the chapter: No More Stage Four

Between my junior and senior years in high school, my parents insisted that I get a summer job to help pay for the escalating expenses of being on the cheerleading squad. I hated to lose those summer days of lazing on the beach all day and partying at night, but I hated the thought of not being a cheerleader even more.

This would be my first foray into the job marketplace. I was completely ignorant of the big bad world that existed beyond the protective limits of my small suburban hometown, El Segundo, California. I halfheartedly submitted some job applications; secretly hoping no offers would be forthcoming. Unfortunately, I received an offer of employment almost immediately. It was from a small factory that laundered linens for the airline industry. My sister, Maureen, had worked for the same outfit a few summers before. She freaked out when I told her about that job offer.

"Absolutely *do not* take that job! You're going to hate it there! You're on your feet for hours; by the end of your shift, your feet and back are going to be killing you. And the women who work there are really mean. Really, really mean. Seriously, do not take that job!"

Frankly, I was a little suspicious of Maureen's motives. At that time, we didn't have a close relationship. It was pretty out of character for her to care about my happiness, or unhappiness, for that matter. I did not heed her warning. Using the excuse that I needed a pair of comfortable shoes because I would be standing for hours, I talked my mom into buying me a new pair of sneakers. Even if the job really sucked, I scored a new pair of shoes.

I arrived early and eager on the first morning of the job. The minute I walked into the warehouse office, my sister's words came back to haunt me. An elderly woman sat hunched behind a dented steel desk, a cigarette dangling precariously between her puckered lips. I smiled and introduced myself. Without speaking a word, she stood up and began marching me through a series of hallways. We finally arrived at the "employee lounge." I use that term loosely. The tables that were scattered around the room were covered with grimy oilcloth tablecloths. The cement floor was so sticky that my shoes made a squelching sound whenever I took a step. The air was thick with cigarette smoke, and all of the ashtrays on the tables were overflowing with cigarette butts. In the corner of the room, a drab avocado-colored refrigerator with a huge dent in the door sent out pitiful sighs and shudders, as though it was on its deathbed. A puddle had formed at the base of the refrigerator; somewhere underneath the dying appliance, water dripped out slowly but steadily. I knew nothing about the mechanics of a refrigerator, but clearly, this refrigerator could not have been doing an adequate job of keeping food items stored at their appropriate temperature. Images of various types of mold I had studied in a science class kept popping up behind my eyes. I just knew that the inside of that refrigerator was a hotbed of spores and other revolting bacteria. I willed myself not to dwell on this, because I had a weak stomach and a hair-trigger gag reflex. There was no way that I would ever open that refrigerator door, much less place any food item of mine in there.

I stood in front of the women clustered around the tables. They glared at me. I definitely sensed hostility in the air.

The supervisor pushed her chair roughly away from the table, stood up, and pointed her finger toward the door that led back into the factory. She wasn't even making eye contact with me when she mumbled, "Follow me." I was anxious to make a hasty retreat from that room, believing that the situation could only improve on the other side of the door. I followed on that woman's heels as closely as those annoying Chihuahua dogs that follow behind you and nip at your heels.

As with the secretary, no words were spoken as we wound our way through the factory. We eventually reached a long row of machines that were about four feet wide and five feet tall. These machines held two huge rollers, one on top of the other, with a small gap between the rollers. I watched the women as they fed large cloth napkins into the space between the rollers. It looked like the machine grabbed the fabric, sucked it in, then hissed out a cloud of steam. After passing through the rollers, the napkin slid out the back of the machine, perfectly flat and steaming hot. I realized this was nothing more than a huge iron. I hated ironing.

The supervisor finally spoke. "This is the mangler." Did I hear her correctly? Did she say *mangler*? As in: "*to mutilate or disfigure by violent tearing or crushing.*" She began yelling out instructions for the mangler. They went like this: Remove the damp clean napkin from basket A. Place the napkin squarely in front of the opening between the two rollers; making sure the napkin is flat and straight when you feed it into the mangler. When the napkin comes out of the other side of the machine, pick it up, fold it, and drop it into basket B.

These instructions were followed by an ominous warning. "Always pay attention! Never look away! Keep your hands away from here!" She was pointing to the place between the two rollers. "If you don't pay attention, this is what happens!" She pulled the hand that had been stuffed into her apron pocket out and thrust it just inches in front of my face. To my horror, she was missing all four of her fingers. She had a thumb but no fingers. She shoved her hand with no fingers back into the apron pocket, and stomped off.

My situation had just gone from enduring a crappy summer job to possibly losing some fingers. In retrospect, I'm amazed that I didn't bolt then and there.

With trembling hands, I fed a napkin into the mangler. I could feel the powerful suction from the rollers, snatching the fabric with a fierceness I had not expected. There was a very definite moment when that machine was going to suck the napkin in, whether you were ready or not, a point of no return. I couldn't imagine how that supervisor had been so distracted that she let her hand get close enough to be yanked into those rollers. The only scenario I could conjure up was that a napkin went through crookedly and she stuck her hand into the rollers to try to pull it back out, sacrificing her fingers for a neatly pressed cloth napkin. There was no chance I would make that mistake.

I cautiously fed another napkin in, but this time the roller sucked it in before I could straighten it out properly. It went through the rollers and came out the other side, literally, mangled. I hadn't been given any instructions on what to do with my misfits, so I tried to hide the napkin in the bottom of the basket. I could hear snickering from the women flanking me. On my third attempt, I very carefully smoothed out the napkin and placed it neatly in front of the rollers. When it came out perfectly pressed, I folded it, set it into my basket, and repeated that process over and over and over again.

Two hours later, at exactly the same moment, the women in the room shut off their manglers and headed toward the employee lounge. I remained at my machine, debating what to do. I sure wasn't going back to the break room. My feet were sore, my back was sore, and my once perky ponytail was sagging and lopsided. I remembered that in front of the factory, there was a row of trees with a short retaining wall beneath them. This would provide the perfect place to escape. I put some change in a vending machine, procured some highly caffeinated soda and sauntered out to the front of the building. Sitting down had never felt so good. It was a beautiful summer day, a perfect day to go to the beach, and I knew that's where most of my friends were. I consoled myself with the fact that my shift ended at 2:30, which meant that I would still have about two hours of beach time. Just thinking about that first dive into the cool waves lifted my misery a little.

When I heard the whirring of the manglers start up, I tried to pull myself together. I applied a fresh coat of lipstick, tightened my ponytail, and then dragged myself back to the factory. When I walked through the door, I could see a small group of women gathered around my machine, pointing at something and whispering in excited murmurs. When they saw me coming, they scattered. Only one person remained: the evil supervisor. She was staring down into my basket of ironed napkins. Before I even reached my machine, she began yelling at me. "Is this all you did? This is ridiculous! You have to do one hundred napkins per hour! Look at the other baskets; you see how full they are? You do one hundred napkins per hour, or you're fired. Do you get that?" Wow. One hundred napkins per hour. She had neglected to mention this quota during my "intro to the mangler course." This was my first day on the job, yet I was expected to keep up with employees who had worked there for many years. I had to smooth, center, iron, and fold a napkin the size of Texas in about forty seconds. Apparently, there was no time allocated for letting the steaming hot napkin cool down for a few seconds. It had occurred to me that I might burn my fingerprints off.

By now all the other women within earshot were laughing at me. I didn't understand why everyone was being so mean to me. Tears began to sting my eyes, so I kept my head down and pretended to focus intently on the next napkin I yanked out of the basket. I gave it a smart snap to add a little drama, and held my breath as the mangler ate it up. My guardian angel must have been on high alert; the napkin slid through the mangler in one fluid movement and came out the other side perfectly pressed. I folded it quickly and gingerly reached down for another napkin. Take that, meanies.

I knew there was no way I could iron the required amount of napkins and keep all of my fingers and my fingerprints. I tried to pick up the pace, stopped fussing so much over every napkin. I folded and added to my basket even the napkins that had been prematurely snatched by the beast and had come out the other side horribly wrinkled. I was betting that nobody was going to go through the stacks of hundreds of napkins in each basket to check for perfection. As the minutes dragged on, I tried to think of ways I could end this misery. Maybe my parents would be satisfied if I toughed it out for three weeks instead of the six I had signed on for. They had been paying for all my cheerleading expenses for three years; maybe I could argue that a precedent had been set. I was an excellent debater.

As the afternoon warmed up, so did the factory. The steam that the machines were puffing out accumulated into the air, hanging oppressively over our heads and making the humidity level skyrocket. Every woman in that building had huge wet rings under their armpits – including me. But at least I had worn deodorant. Others evidently had not, and the room reeked so badly that I finally took a napkin and tied it over my face so that I wasn't inhaling the stench that enveloped the room. My co-workers looked perplexed. I think they had built up a tolerance to the stink.

When my next break rolled around, I hit the vending machine with a vengeance. I bought two sodas this time because I needed to pump as much caffeine into my bloodstream as possible, and potato chips to replenish the salt I was losing from sweating like a marathon runner. I walked back out to the retaining wall in front of the building, but this time there were a handful of Hispanic men sitting on the grass beneath the shade of a huge oak tree. When they noticed me standing across from them, they all smiled. Not normal, how are you doing smiles, but creepy, lustful smiles. Within seconds, the catcalls and sleazy Spanish expressions drifted across the hot summer air toward me. One of the men put his first and second finger in the configuration of the victory or peace sign up to his mouth and then wiggled his tongue between his two fingers. I was such an innocent, I had no idea what this meant – but I knew it was dirty because the men howled at the sight. Horrified, I turned and began a hasty retreat. I could hear the men continue to yell as I walked away. "Hey mommeee, come back." I broke into a sprint.

I hid on the side of the building. I had to sit on the grass but at least I was in a shady spot. My body ached from head to toe and my clothes were sticking to me. I had a headache from wearing my very thick hair in a ponytail for too long, and I was getting the shakes from drinking too much caffeine. I had to be honest with myself – there was no way I would last even three weeks in this God-forsaken place. I yanked my hair back up into a ponytail and plodded back to the factory with as much enthusiasm as an inmate walking the Green Mile.

From across the room, I could see that the women were gathered around my machine. The evil supervisor was holding a mangled napkin in her hand. OH NO! She had gone through my basket and pulled out all the misfits. There were a lot of misfits. My shakes intensified. She yelled across the room, "What is wrong with you?" This can't go to out to a customer!" I just couldn't face another tongue lashing and more public humiliation. I figured I was going to get fired anyway, so I decided I would beat her to the punch. I calmly turned around and began meandering toward the exit. The evil supervisor began to semi-trot in my direction. "Hey! Your break is over! Where do you think you're going?" I panicked and began thinking crazy thoughts. What if she tried to keep me here against my will? What if she held me hostage and shackled me to a mangler machine and made me iron for hours? (I've always had a vivid imagination.) I broke into a sprint and raced out the door that led to my freedom. I had so much adrenaline running through my blood, I think I ran full speed for about five blocks, glancing back over my shoulder every few seconds to make sure the evil supervisor wasn't chasing me.

I lived on the other side of town, about a mile walk. On this day, with the sun beating down mercilessly on my back and my head and feet throbbing, it was an agonizing walk.

I must have been quite a sight when I walked across our front yard. My mom had been gardening, but she dropped the trowel that she had been using and stood up when she saw me. "Why are you home so early? What happened to you?" My socks had disappeared into my shoes. My shorts were halfway up my crotch, my ponytail was now a low bun, and my blouse was stuck to me because I was soaked in sweat.

I collapsed onto the grass and burst into tears. "They were so awful, mommy! All of the women were really mean, nobody would talk to me; they laughed at me and made fun of me! And the supervisor was really mean and she kept screaming at me all day long! There were some guys that said dirty things to me in Spanish! And they did this," at which point I imitated the victory sign over the open lips with wagging tongue sticking out. A very subtle but undeniable flicker of horror crossed my mother's face. "I don't even know what that means! Do you?" Without missing a beat, my mom said, "It means you're never going back to that place."

Years later, I came to understand that I had done a very brief stint in a sweatshop. The women who were mean to me were prisoners trapped in a dead end job with no hope that anything better might come along. In order to survive, they worked for minimum wage with no rights and no benefits, in an environment that was filthy and hazardous. I was just a rich kid, who stopped by for a few weeks to make some pocket change, and then I would skip back to my wonderful, carefree world, a world these people had no hope of ever entering. Up until that day, I had no idea that there were people in the United States of America living in abject poverty and despair.

■ ■

I realize you're wondering what any of this has to do with breast cancer. I won't keep you in suspense. Because there is a history of breast cancer in my family, I began having mammograms in my late thirties. The first time I walked into a room where a mammogram machine stood, I froze in my tracks. This piece of equipment bore a frightening resemblance to *the mangler*. There were two pieces of glass that could be cranked open or clamped shut. After the technician was done contorting me into a Quasimodo-like position, my breasts were lifted and slapped down onto the lower piece of glass, and then rudely manipulated like they were a piece of raw meat. This was followed by the two glass plates being slowly adjusted until my breast was painfully compressed into the shape of a shark fin. This machine was the mangler, and my breast was the napkin being ironed flat!

I loathed having my annual mammogram, not just because of the physical discomfort, but because memories of that harrowing experience at the sweatshop came flooding back. I would sink into a sad, depressed state for days. Was this some form of PTSD?

Breast cancer is the most commonly diagnosed cancer among American women.

In 2021, an estimated 281,550 new cases of breast cancer are expected to be diagnosed in the United States. About 43,600 women are expected to die from breast cancer.

Recent research involving more than 50,000 breast cancer patients found that those who took part in a breast cancer-screening program had a sixty per cent lower risk of dying from the disease in the ten years after diagnosis, and forty seven per cent had a lower risk twenty years after diagnosis.

A woman's risk of breast cancer nearly doubles if she has a first degree relative (mother, sister, daughter) who has been diagnosed with breast cancer.

Mammograms are proven to reduce mammogram deaths.

If every woman would be vigilant about having an annual mammogram, we could wipe out stage four cancer.

Being familiar with most of the above statistics, I had a mammogram every single year for many, many years. Then, one year, I skipped it. I skipped the following year, too. Almost three years had passed before I finally had a mammogram. That long overdue mammogram saved my life.

THIS IS BAD

Moral of the chapter: Follow your survival instincts

It was early December 2011, when I had that mammogram done. A few days later I received a letter from a radiologist advising me that I needed to schedule a repeat mammogram and an ultrasound of my breasts. The reasons given were vague, something about possible abnormalities. I had received this sort of letter a few times in the past, but nothing ever came of it. Invariably, I was always given a clean bill of health. Because this particular mammogram was so overdue this letter brought with it an uneasy feeling. I immediately called the breast imaging center where my prior follow up mammograms had been done. Throughout the three day wait before the follow up mammogram, I checked my breasts again and again for any kind of lump. I felt nothing at all.

I had never asked my husband, Michael, to come with me to any of these follow-up appointments. This time, I did.

We arrived on time for my two o'clock appointment. The large waiting room was packed, but my name was called almost immediately. The receptionist led me down a series of corridors that led to the dressing rooms. I put on a hospital gown, and was then escorted down more corridors to where the mammogram beast awaited.

The technician was standing behind a Plexiglas-enclosed area. This was where the motherboard that controlled the mammogram was located. She was fiddling with some knobs and didn't bother to look up when I walked in.

From across the room, still not making eye contact, she mumbled, "Remove your right arm from the gown and step in front of the machine."

The films from my initial mammogram were clipped to a light box mounted on the wall. The technician studied them intently before she stepped out from behind the glass and began the long, uncomfortable process of getting my boob into the perfect placement. Her instructions were curt, and her hands were ice cold.

She stepped back to the operating panel and took a picture. She walked back to me, contorted me a little more, and took another picture. This pattern was repeated again and again. The amount of views she was imaging far exceeded any prior mammograms I had undergone. I didn't want to freak out, but it was impossible not to acknowledge that something was wrong.

My entire breast was bright red from being smooshed between the glass plates. The pain from this process had radiated and was now shooting in excruciating spasms into my upper back. I bit my lip and began to softly whimper.

Finally, I was told I could step back and put my gown on, but I was to remain standing in front of the machine. The technician grabbed my mammogram films and quickly exited the room.

I could hear a discussion going on in the adjoining room. The voices were too muffled to understand the words that were being spoken, but their tone was definitely tense.

When the technician returned to the room, she said she needed to take a few more pictures. I stepped forward, but as soon as she began to maneuver my unspeakably tender breast, I began to whimper loudly. I couldn't help it. When she lowered the glass, I started to yell, "Ooow, ooow, ooow"...... She took two quick pictures, told me I could put my gown back on but again asked that I remain standing in front of the machine. The ensuing argument from the adjacent room added to my rapidly rising panic.

I disobediently left my post and walked over to the light box where my films were hanging. X-rays are fairly easy to read, but I had no idea how to interpret these images. I stared at what appeared to be the outline of a very large shark fin, (that would be my breast being compressed as flat as a pancake.) Other than that, I had no idea what I was looking at.

When I heard fast footsteps in the corridor, I scooted across the room toward the mammogram beast. The technician stormed past me in quite a state. Her shoulders were hunched forward, lips pursed tightly; her face flushed a bright red. Apparently, someone had just given her a verbal ass-kicking. She snapped at me. "I told you to stay in place! Get back in place! And hurry up!" She was huffing like a bull as she slapped at the knobs on the control panel.

Normally, I would have just kept my mouth shut and complied with the order. I'm much more likely to walk away from an offensive remark (and cry in another room) than to stand my ground or defend myself. But I was petrified. I could be minutes away from being diagnosed with a life threatening disease. I deserved to be treated with a modicum of compassion and patience. On this afternoon, I listened to that voice in my head urging me to speak up. *Stand up for yourself. Don't let her speak to you like that.*

I turned around to face her. "How long have you been a mammogram technician?"

She looked up at me, pausing for a moment before she said, "About two years."

"Okay, then. I've been having mammograms for like, 20 years, and I have *never ever* had to have so many films taken during a session. So, if you're not a trainee and you know what you're doing, then I have to assume that you think you see some kind of breast cancer." I spoke quickly, so that she couldn't interrupt me. "I worked in the medical profession for many years. I know that you're not supposed to discuss any diagnostic findings with me, but I refuse to have one more view taken until I know what's going on. If you can't tell me, you better go find someone who can."

No smiling, no waffling, no sweetness and light. I felt so I empowered. I felt like a different person. I liked that person!

Her expression and her voice softened immediately. "I'm sorry. You have two spots at the very back of your breast. They're almost against the muscle tissue that runs behind your breast. This is a really hard area to image. I have to keep taking views until I can get some clear pictures of those areas."

OMG. She never used the word cancer, but it was definitely implied. Not just a little tiny spot of cancer, but two spots. Two spots that were way back by my muscle tissue, meaning the cancer may have spread into my muscle or even my bones. I WANT MY MOMMY!

"Oh. Okay. Thank you." I stepped back and placed myself in front of the machine. I couldn't stop the flow of tears that had begun to run down my cheeks.

She gently maneuvered my raw red breast onto the lower glass, and then, millimeters at a time, began cranking the upper glass down. She began encouraging me. "I'm sorry, it's almost over. You're doing great." I began doing the panting I had learned in Lamaze class. Mercifully, it was only a matter of minutes before she said, " That's it! I got it! "

I pulled my gown back on, and we walked the short distance to the adjoining ultrasound room. The walk took much longer than it should have because I was taking baby steps. I put one hand under my breast to stabilize it, because even the slightest bounce was agonizing.

While I was waiting in the ultrasound room, I noticed that against one wall was a long counter that displayed a variety of informative pamphlets. The topics covered every aspect of breast cancer. I began to shake uncontrollably. Even my teeth were chattering.

The ultrasound technician slid softly into the room, her tiny white nurse shoes making a muffled whooshing sound preceding her arrival. She introduced herself as Mona. When she saw the state I was in, she set her clipboard down and came over to comfort me. She picked up one of my hands and cradled it between her own warm, soft hands. I wanted to tuck into her, to lay my head down on her shoulder and howl out my terror.

Mona knew exactly what to say. "It's going to be okay. Do you know how many of these tests we do every single day? Eighty percent of the patients do not have cancer. What we see on your mammogram films could be any number of things. I know you're scared but try not to jump to the very worst conclusion. Let's just take this one step at a time."

I took a deep breath and exhaled slowly. When I calmed down, Mona said, "I'm going to go get you a warm blanket before we start the test. I'll be right back." Before she left the room, she handed me a big box of unopened Kleenex.

She returned with a blanket fresh out of the dryer, deliciously warm. I wanted to pull it over my head so that I could block out the monster that I knew was there in the room with us.

Before she began, Mona asked me if I had ever had an ultrasound test. I told her that I had gone through many ultrasounds and had a very good understanding of how the test worked.

This is what a breast ultrasound test involves:

The first step in this process is having a thick gel applied over your entire breast. This gel assists in transmitting sound waves. Sitting on a portable table next to the patient's bed is a keyboard, along with a small piece of equipment that resembles a TV monitor.

The technician uses a small, hand held electronic device that looks like a wand. As it glides over your breast, it sends images of the tissue underneath to the monitor screen. The technician begins with wide swaths and gentle pressure to hone in on the exact spot of concern, watching the monitor to observe the images projected there.

It was only a matter of seconds before Mona zeroed in on one particular area; she began to glide the wand over that area again and again, increasing the pressure of the wand more and more. She began making clicking sounds with the wand, which meant that she was now taking pictures of something. She spoke to me throughout the test in a soothing tone of voice.

After finding the exact location, Mona told me to turn my head so that I could see the images on the screen that was a few feet away from my shoulders. When she pressed the wand firmly against my breast at about the 9:00 position, the image that appeared surprised me. I was expecting to see something like an X-ray or MRI image, something one dimensional with stark black and white contrasts. Instead, what appeared on the monitor resembled a shallow, slow moving wave. The image was alive. When Mona would press down against my breast, the tissue would undulate lazily. It didn't take long for me to spot the troublemakers.

Appearing insidiously innocuous were two very small spots, stationary and opaque, that looked like two tiny islands. The first spot was about one inch long and very thin, maybe one eighth of an inch. There was a space of about half an inch, and then the second spot, which was shaped the same, but much smaller.

"This is what we've been looking for, right here."

Those two little spots? How serious could they be?

Mona set the wand down next to the monitor, and said, "OK, this is what happens next. You will need to come back for a needle biopsy. This is standard procedure, just a way for us to gather more information on those spots we see. The biopsy is very quick, and not painful. A very tiny needle is inserted into the areas we are concerned about, and fluid is drawn out. A pathologist will examine this fluid, and be able to tell us if these spots are benign or malignant. Then we take it from there. Remember, 80% of these tests come back benign."

"Let me just check the schedule. I'll be right back."

I could hear Mona speaking to another person in an adjoining office. The voices were going back and forth in a tight, tense volley.

Suddenly, the door was slammed open, and a very tall, thin woman burst into the room.

She raced across the room on spindly, spidery legs without even looking in my direction. With her back to me, she bent over and stared intently at some of the ultrasound images. She turned around after a time, and roughly yanked at the blanket that was tucked around me, exposing my right breast. She continued to focus on the screen as she began making passes with the wand over my breast. I noticed that Mona was sort of huddled over in the corner of the room, with a "deer caught in the headlights" expression on her face.

The woman straightened up and barked over at me, "I'm Dr. Jones, Head of Radiology."

She turned to face Mona and snapped, "When did you say the first availability for a needle biopsy was?" Mona seemed to implode, making her body as small as possible, crossing her arms in front of herself and staring down at the floor. "The next available needle biopsy is not until Tuesday afternoon." Today was Thursday. Mona had barely gotten the words out of her mouth when Dr. Jones bellowed, "Well, that will not do!" I could hardly believe my eyes when I saw her pitch the wand that she had been holding across the room. It hit the countertop with a sharp clatter, and then did a few cartwheels before skidding to a stop.

I was shocked. Never in my life had I seen a doctor display such obnoxious behavior. I started to plot an escape route out of the room.

Dr. Jones began to run her fingers through her hair. Suddenly, she exclaimed, "Alright! Let's just do this right now! Get a technician in here. We're going to get this done right now."

Mona was still crouching over in the corner, staring at the floor. I think she was afraid to make eye contact with the doctor. (You know that theory about not making eye contact with a wild animal because they interpret it as a sign of aggression and it may provoke them to attack? Well, Mona was not taking any chances.) Speaking barely above a whisper, she said, "It's after five o'clock, Dr. Jones. The technicians have all left for the day."

Mona and I both shrank back a little, knowing that Dr. Jones wasn't going to take this well. I couldn't bear to see Mona subjected to the doctor's wrath, so I created a diversion. I scooted to the edge of the table, held my gown tightly around me, and placed my feet flat on the ground, just in case I needed to bolt. I stared at the wall in front of me and asked nobody in particular, "Is there something really wrong?" I hadn't realized how dry my mouth was until I spoke those words and my upper lip stuck above my teeth.

Dr. Jones glared in my direction and let out a little huff of disgust. I will remember her reply for the rest of my life. Ver batim, this is what she said: "Well, I don't know if there is something *really* wrong! But look at this!" She stomped over to the monitor, and pointed to my two little islands. "See this? This is bad! This is very bad!" She might as well have just screamed out, "YOU HAVE CANCER AND YOU MIGHT DIE!"

For the second time that afternoon, that other persona that had been dormant my entire life took charge. I stood up and stepped away from the exam table, crossed my arms over my chest, and looked directly into a pair of beady little eyes. I cleared my throat to make sure I didn't have any froggies that would make me sound less fierce.

"Dr. Jones, I don't have any idea what that means. You're going to have to be much more specific than that."

Dr. Jones rolled her eyes and made another little huffing noise. I was irritating her. "Well, I cannot say for *certain* that it is cancer. BUT IT LOOKS VERY BAD!" Nope, not good enough.

"Yes, I get that, Dr. Jones. I get that it looks *very bad*. What I would like to know, specifically, is if you think I have cancer."

She squinted over toward the ultrasound monitor.

"Have you ever had serious injuries to your chest area? Like, been in a car accident that involved injuries to your chest area?"

"No."

"Well then, I think you have breast cancer."

****

I was in such a hurry to get out of that building that I stuffed my bra into my purse and only buttoned the first three buttons on my blouse. I didn't slow down when I reached the reception area. Michael was sitting on the edge of his chair, looking very concerned.

I'm sure he could tell by the state I was in that things had not gone well.

He jumped up as soon as he saw me and began asking, "What took so long? What's going on?"

I didn't do anything to soften the blow, I just blurted it out: "I have breast cancer."

There were a few seconds of stunned silence before he began peppering me with questions. "What? You have *breast cancer?* They actually said, '*you have breast cancer*'?" The organic chemist in my husband was immediately suspicious. He knew that many diagnostic tests have to be performed before a patient is told they have cancer.

"No. They said, they *think* I have breast cancer."

"How can they possibly *think* that you have breast cancer? You've only had two tests, and they're both preliminary. They can't possibly know that you have breast cancer until you've had more diagnostic tests. This is crazy!"

I could sense Michael was panicking, clutching at straws. I think subconsciously he was presenting this argument to give me, and himself, a few more days of hope. He was angry that anyone would give me a premature diagnosis. This served no purpose except to terrorize us until my cancer was confirmed, at which time we could rightfully freak out.

"And anyway, who said you have breast cancer?"

"The Head of Radiology. She didn't want to tell me, but the tests were taking so long and I knew something was really wrong and I just wanted to know the truth. I sort of forced her to tell me."

"The Head of Radiology?" That stopped him short.

"Honey, I want to go home."

Human beings are hard wired for survival. We've all read accounts of ordinary people doing extraordinary things: the woman who lifts a car up because her child is trapped beneath it; the soldier who carries four injured comrades out of battle and into safety; the surfer who fends off a great white shark by punching it in the snout. This phenomenon is known as hysterical strength. There is a second type of survival instinct that we rely on much more frequently. This is called the fight-or-flight response. When we are feeling very stressed out, our brain interprets this as being in a dangerous situation. Our bodies undergo a series of chemical releases and nerve cell responses. A gland in our brain, the hypothalamus, sets off some triggers. Adrenaline is released into our bloodstream. This causes our pulse to become rapid and our heart rate to increase. Blood is pumped more quickly into our muscles and limbs. Awareness, sight, and impulses intensify and quicken. When your boss is chewing you out in front of a group of co-workers, or a creepy guy is walking too closely behind you, your fight or flight survival instinct will engage.

That afternoon at the breast diagnostic center, my survival instincts kicked in, and I had listened to them and let them take over. Throughout my cancers, I learned to rely heavily on those instincts. They became my battle armor, not protecting me from bullets or swords but from intangible things that were just as lethal - like very bad medical advice. They encouraged me to speak up; they caused me to be my own patient advocate.

If you are battling cancer, give in to your gut feelings. If things don't sound right or feel right, ask questions. Bottom line; learn to recognize and trust your survival instincts.

THE DEGENERES DEBACLE

Moral of the Chapter: Let Go, Or Be Dragged

Yes, I realize everybody loves Ellen DeGeneres. I love her, too. In fact, the first thing I did when Michael and I returned home from the breast diagnostic center was Google my way to The Ellen Show website. It was mid-November, so the Twelve Days of Christmas were about to begin. For the dozen or so of you who don't watch the show, being in the audience of The Ellen Show during the Twelve Days of Christmas is like hitting a jackpot in Vegas. Those in attendance are showered with amazing gifts, like vacations and state–of–the-art electronics. I was desperate to get into one of those audiences, but not for the reason you would think. At that time I had no idea what stage or type of breast cancer I had. I didn't even know if my life was going to come to a very early end. It didn't escape me that receiving a boatload of presents might not be exciting if I weren't around to enjoy them. It wasn't the gifts that I was after.

If you have ever watched an episode of The Ellen Show, you have seen miracles and wishes come true. You have seen people who are living or have lived through tragic events be lifted out of their misery, and given hope and relief through Ellen's generosity. There is usually some segment of her show that makes me cry, the good kind of crying, the crying because my heart feels so full of love. The Ellen Show provided me with one hour out of every day that was guaranteed to make me laugh and cry, to lift my spirits, and to help me keep my own problems in perspective.

I needed to get on that show because I saw it as the perfect escape from the terror I was feeling. I believed that sitting in an audience full of people who were immersed in the holiday spirit and giddy with Christmas cheer would transport me out of my horrifying situation. It might just be for a few brief hours, but those few brief hours would have been a Godsend to me.

I clicked on the link that allowed me to send a message to The Ellen Show producers. I wrote that I had just been diagnosed with breast cancer, that I was terrified, and that I **really** wanted to be in the audience on any of the Twelve Days of Christmas. I received no reply to that email.

About a week later I received an e-mail announcing that The Ellen Show was about to launch a contest that would allow winners to be in the audience for one of the Twelve Days of Christmas. I clicked on that link and read the contest rules. The entrant was required to submit an eight-hundred word essay on why they should be selected to be in the audience. I had to think about that for a minute. There were thousands of fans that would be entering the contest, and I knew that a diagnosis of breast cancer might be pretty low on the list of heartbreaks or catastrophes other viewers had experienced.

 Over the years, on five different occasions, I had submitted a column to our local newspaper, *The Daily Breeze*. Once a week this newspaper would print a column that had been written by a reader, just regular folk who were hoping to get their five minutes of fame and twenty-five bucks. (Actually I don't think the money was a big motivator. I think it was more the fame part.) Circulation for the paper was 76,618, and I had no idea how many submissions were received on a daily basis or what my chances were of getting published. After hesitating for months, I finally took the plunge and submitted my first column. My submission was chosen and printed on December 23, 2005.

I felt like a superstar when I saw my column in the newspaper! The exhilaration and pride was exactly what I needed to convince myself that I was actually capable of writing something worth reading. The following year, a column that I submitted in late November was chosen and printed on Christmas Day. Definitely one of the best presents I've ever received! I had since submitted three more columns, and each time, my submissions were printed. With this in mind, I sat down at my laptop and wrote my essay. After several rewrites, I said a prayer and hit send to The Ellen Show.

I received nothing more than an automatic thank you as a reply. Since the contest continued to run and a new winner was chosen every day, I submitted another essay. Again, I received an automatic thank you and nothing more.

I gave it a third try. By now, my confidence was shot and I was beginning to feel bitter. It really hurt to read those cold, automatic thank you emails. Rejection is always hard to face, but I was so vulnerable at that time, these rejections felt brutal.

I was not invited to attend any of The Twelve Days of Christmas shows.

This is the picture I sent to the Ellen Show.

A normal person probably would have given up any attempt to get into that Ellen audience, but I turned it into a mission. Since my goal was not to obtain awesome prizes but to merely be at a taping, I signed up for tickets to be in the audience. Initially, this seemed very promising. I chose dates that were months away, and according to the website, still had openings in those audiences. I was now on The Ellen Show email list, so I received notices whenever there were additional opportunities to be at a taping. I always took the bait, with no success.

My diagnosis of thyroid cancer brought even more urgency to get in that audience. Again, it wasn't the prizes I was after. I had convinced myself that some kind of magic would rub off on me if I could only get close enough to Ellen. I thought the joy and zany energy from the audience would bring me some kind of healing. I began contacting the producers immediately after my diagnosis, believing that surely two cancers in two years would get me into that audience. I continued to enter all the contests and sign up for tickets to be in the audience. Even after my skin cancer diagnosis, three cancers in three consecutive years, I could not get the attention of anyone associated with that show.

And then one evening, I received a phone call from a young woman who identified herself as someone calling on behalf of The Ellen Show. The minute I heard those three words, my heart began to beat wildly against my chest. Unfortunately, this young woman was not calling to offer me tickets to be in the audience. She was calling to offer me tickets to a new game show that I think was a new business venture for Ellen. Ellen herself would not personally be appearing on this new game show.

A tsunami of panic swept over me. I had been trying for three years, and I knew this would be the best opportunity I would ever get to be in the Ellen audience. I explained to the young woman that I was not interested in tickets to the new game show, but that I had been trying for three years to get on The Ellen Show. I told her of my three battles with cancer. She was very sympathetic, but advised me that she could be of no help because she didn't have anything to do with getting on The Ellen Show; she was just trying to scare up an audience for the new game show. She encouraged me to send an email to the producers; she was certain that after they heard my story, I would get tickets to the show. I told her that I had already tried that route many, many times, that I had signed up for tickets for three years, that I had entered every contest that came down the pike. Nothing was working. By then I was crying. I could hear the desperation in my voice "Oh, you should try again!" I pleaded with her to at least take my name and phone number and try to get my information into the hands of anyone affiliated with The Ellen Show. She declined to do that, telling me once again-still in a very sweet voice-that she had no connection with that show and that I should try (again) to contact Ellen through her website. And then she hung up. She actually hung up on me!

When I heard the sound of the dial tone, I knew I would never be on The Ellen Show. I had tried every conceivable method, and it had all been an effort in futility. I slid down to the kitchen floor, still clutching the phone in my hand. I sat there for a few minutes, bawling my eyes out. And then I got up and got a Popsicle.

That phone call turned out to be blessing in disguise. It made me realize that it was time for me to let go---or be dragged. I was unnecessarily subjecting myself to rejection and sadness. I was beating my head against a wall. I was wasting whatever precious energy I had left. I longed to be in the Ellen audience, to feel that healing, happy energy, but it just wasn't meant to be.

I still receive emails from The Ellen Show, enticing me to enter this contest or that. My survival instincts prevent me from clicking on those emails; they whisper in my ear that I will be opening the door to Loserville. I have a little scar on my heart from that horrible experience, of trying so hard but getting nowhere. If I'm philosophical about it, compared to all my other scars, it's pretty insignificant. But for some reason, it doesn't feel that way.

DO YOUR HOMEWORK

Moral of the Chapter: Knowledge is Power

The day I received my breast cancer diagnosis, Michael immersed himself in research. He studied every aspect of my type and stage of cancer. He scrutinized graphs, charts, statistics, and current medical publications on cancer research. He educated himself on every diagnostic test involved and how to interpret the results. He delved into surgical options. He familiarized himself with the complex pharmacology of chemotherapy; the different types of drugs commonly used and what side effects to expect. Lastly, he took on radiation therapy and everything that involved. We had an awesome advantage throughout this crisis: Michael has a PhD in organic chemistry. He actually understood everything he was reading, and he was able to translate this information into layman's terms so that I could understand it, too.

For my part, I was mostly researching support groups. I wanted to know what the journey had been like for other women. I wanted to be prepared for whatever lay ahead. The Internet is flooded with legitimate breast cancer websites, but I learned that there are also a boat-load of bogus sites. These sites are merely opinions or observations, not based in fact or medical science. Don't go there- it might do more harm than good. Check the URL at the top of your computer screen to make sure you haven't been misdirected to a bogus site.

If we had not done all this research, this homework, there's no doubt in my mind that I would have had an unnecessary mastectomy, possibly a double mastectomy.

In late December, we met with a breast surgeon. I insisted Michael be able to come into the exam room with me for two reasons: I needed the emotional support, and if the surgeon started spewing complex medical jargon, I needed Michael to translate. I removed my blouse and bra, put on one of those ridiculous paper gowns, and hopped on to the examining table. When the doctor waltzed in with my chart under his arm, he introduced himself, and got right down to business. He uncovered my breasts and did a brief physical exam. Without bothering to close the flimsy paper gown, he stepped back and announced "OK, Melissa, I've read your tests results. I think a mastectomy is the best course of treatment for you."

Michael and I had done extensive research on mastectomies and lumpectomies. (Skip forward to chapter six if you don't know the difference between the two.) According to every article we read, I should have been an excellent candidate for a lumpectomy. I was literally dumbstruck. My husband was not.

"Doctor, I'm confused. I have a PhD in organic chemistry, and I've done a lot of research on Melissa's cancer. Everything that I have read has led me to believe that Melissa would be a viable candidate for a lumpectomy."

The doctor took umbrage at this challenge.

"Hmff…. Well, no, that would never work in her situation. Look at all that breast tissue! She has far too much breast tissue!"

Michael continued, "I'm confused. Doesn't a lot of breast tissue make her a *good* candidate for a lumpectomy?"

"No, it does not. It's far too much work." With a look of horror/disgust on his face, he pointed to me and exclaimed, "Look at the size of her breasts! No surgeon is going to want to deal with all that! That is way too much flesh!" He was practically shuddering. I was still lying down on the exam table, the paper gown crinkled up under my armpits, boobs totally exposed. Upon hearing his words, I shot up on the exam table and covered my chest.

Michael continued on. "OK, well, let's say Melissa has a mastectomy. What would we be looking at as far as reconstructive surgery?"

"That's not my specialty. You would see a plastic surgeon for that. But most of the patients that I've treated that are Melissa's age, in her situation, usually don't even bother with that. You've been married for a long time, right? In a stable relationship? Most women don't bother doing anything after surgery."

What did he mean, patients my age? I was in my fifties! Yes, I was in a stable relationship, but what did that have to do with anything? If it wasn't absolutely necessary, I didn't want to live out the rest of my life hooterless. If my life were at risk, I would have given up my girls without hesitation. But that wasn't the case.

I looked over at Michael. He was speechless, too, but not for long.

"Doctor, let me make sure I am understanding you. You are telling us that Melissa should have a mastectomy because she has too much breast tissue. It has nothing to do with her type or stage or location of cancer---she just has too much breast tissue." Even though Michael asked this in a very calm tone, the doctor took umbrage that anyone would question his opinion. Or, maybe he realized that we understood what he was *really* saying.

Sputter, sputter. "Well, yes, that is absolutely true! You're not going to find a breast surgeon who will be willing to work with all that breast tissue! It's too much work! She could have a mastectomy in about two hours, but a lumpectomy could take—he glanced over at me—five hours!" He stomped over to the door, flung it open, and shouted into the hallway, "DID ANYONE TAKE THIS PATIENT'S WEIGHT?"

OMG. Absolute, unadulterated, utter humiliation. Never in my life have I wanted to bitch slap anyone the way I wanted to bitch slap that doctor. I could feel my heart beating against my chest as I prayed that nobody would shout out the answer to that question. (Thank God, nobody did.)

That was the tipping point for Michael. He already had some serious reservations about this surgeon. He was suspect of the doctor's medical opinion, and uncomfortable with how defensive he became when he was asked a question or challenged in any way. That unconscionable, unbelievably unprofessional act of bellowing out into the hallway to get my weight made the decision to scratch this surgeon off our list of possible candidates a no brainer.

From across the room, I heard Michael softly say, "Melissa, get dressed. We're through here." He shot the doctor the stink eye, I pulled my blouse on, and we made a dash for the door. We may have left skid marks.

The entire drive home, foul words were spewing non-stop from Michael's mouth. He has a huge vocabulary of vile language: he unleashed every bad word known to mankind; he might have even made up a few new ones. He kept repeating again and again that he just did not believe that I needed a mastectomy. He started quoting facts that he had read while doing research on my cancer. I sat silent; the scenario of the doctor hollering out for my weight was running through my mind in an endless loop. Oh, the mortification. As we pulled into our driveway, Michael said, "Honey, I'm so sorry that you had to go through that. That doctor is a disgrace to his profession. He should have his license revoked. We're going to find you a great doctor, and you're not going to have a mastectomy."

As a side note, we found out that three women had recently filed complaints against this doctor for making derogatory comments about their weight. What an ass clown.

We soldiered on in our search for a breast surgeon. Our second choice was a physician who was affiliated with a prestigious California university. I was afraid when I called to make an appointment that I was going to have to wait weeks to get in, but the medical receptionist was exceedingly kind and understanding. It may have helped that I was crying as I tried to explain my situation and my feeling of urgency to see a doctor. Because I had copies of all of my lab work and diagnostic tests, I was able to get an appointment almost immediately.

On a sunny morning in early January, Michael and I headed down the 405 Freeway with a renewed hope. We bungled our way through the university campus until we found the right building, and then the right office. Michael and I were escorted into an exam room and given no instructions whatsoever. I was not asked to remove my clothing, I was not even asked to sit up on the exam table. So I didn't. I sat in one of the two chairs that were placed against the wall, figuring that when the doctor came in, she would ask me to sit up on the exam table. When she did walk into the room a few moments later, she, herself, sat up on the exam table.

She walked directly over to me, shook my hand, and hopped up on the exam table, sitting sidesaddle. She completely ignored Michael. After flipping through my chart very briefly, she closed it, and set it down next to her. She launched into a lecture about breast cancer. I could tell by the way she droned on in a monotonous tone that she must have repeated this little lecture to every new patient. If she had opened the conversation by asking me how much I knew about my condition, we could have skipped her entire diatribe and jumped right into her diagnosis. I walked into that appointment really hoping that this would be the right surgeon for me. The sooner I had the surgery, the sooner I could move on to necessary follow up therapies, and the sooner I would be cancer free. I kept trying to spot something encouraging about her, some positive quality in her facial expressions or body language, anything. I was drawing a blank. That's the vibe I felt; blank. Empty. Cold. Detached. As the minutes ticked by, she was sitting up on that examining table, yakking away, staring at a poster hanging about two feet over my head.

This type of doctor should be avoided at all costs. They do not see you as a person, a human being, a living thing–they see you as a number. Their focus is on determining a diagnosis, deciding on a course of treatment, executing that treatment, and hopefully, never seeing you again.

My heart sank when the doctor wound down her long-winded lecture by telling us that she believed a mastectomy was the best course of treatment. The minute I heard that, I began to feel anxious and nauseous. It became difficult for me to focus on anything she was saying. This is exactly why you should never go to a doctor's appointment without bringing a friend or relative. Somebody has to pay attention and take notes because you're probably not going to able to.

The doctor was finally forced to acknowledge that Michael was in the room because as soon as he found an opening in the thus far one-way conversation, he began to pepper her with questions. I think this was only tolerated because Michael began by giving her a brief synopsis of his educational background. Her attitude changed significantly.

The argument she presented was that my cancer had a high rate of recurrence, and if I opted for a lumpectomy, I would be running the risk of needing a second surgery a few years down the road. When asked about the strategy for reconstructive surgery, she had the same answer as the previous doctor. That is, reconstructive surgery was not her specialty; I would need to make an appointment with a plastic surgeon to have any of those types of questions answered. Michael asked her if she would be meeting with my plastic surgeon before my surgery, in order to put in place a game plan for reconstruction prior to the removal of my breast. She waved her hand dismissively and said that was not really necessary. She even took it a step farther by suggesting that the best option for me would be to have both breasts removed. If I only had one breast removed, the surgeon was going to have to do a breast reduction on my healthy breast, so that I had a matched set. It would be easier for the plastic surgeon to start with a clean slate.

There were two major flaws in her argument. She had said that my cancer had a high rate of recurrence as if that were a statement of fact. It was not. The recurrence rate of breast cancer is based primarily on your onco (oncology) score. Your onco score is based on genetic tests of samples of the cancerous tumor that are taken during surgery. You do not know what the risk of recurrence for your cancer is until *after* surgery.

Secondly, for all her fancy footwork, this doctor was really saying that it was easier *for the surgical team* to just remove both breasts. She was not saying that I needed my breast(s) removed due to elements of my cancer. And here was the best part: a mastectomy was an outpatient procedure. That's right. Drop by the hospital in the morning, we'll lop your hooters off, and you can leave that same afternoon. I was shocked. "Wait, what? You remove a woman's breast and send her home the same day? That doesn't sound right. I don't want to go home the same day my breasts are removed!"

"Most insurances will not cover an overnight stay."

That also sounded like a statement of fact and in the moment, I didn't have enough wits about me to question that statement. Michael and I had done plenty of research on breast cancer, but we had neglected to research what the state laws were pertaining to breast cancer surgery and related associated treatments. When we got home that night, it took me about five minutes on the internet to discover her statement that "most insurances will not cover an overnight stay" was flat out wrong. The law stated that the physician, surgeon, and patient made a joint decision on a hospital stay. Furthermore, the law provided that if hospitalization was required, the insurance provider could not require the physician to get pre-authorization.

I don't understand how this physician could have been so ignorant about California state laws governing breast cancer.

(Down the road, when I met with the plastic surgeon who would be reconstructing my breasts, I made it very clear that I wanted to be hospitalized overnight. It was an hour drive from our home to Hoag Hospital, and that was if there was no traffic on the freeway. I thought it was safer for me to spend the night at the hospital. My doctor agreed. My insurance provider covered the stay, no questions asked.)

I was feeling sicker by the minute. Fortunately, a nurse stuck her head in the door at about that time, signaling that it was time for the doctor to move on to her next patient. I shoved the list of pre-surgery tests she had handed me into my purse.

As soon as we got home, Michael went back online to review, again, all the information he had read about my cancer. A few hours later, he walked into the living room and announced, "That doctor is wrong. You do not need a mastectomy. We're going to keep looking."

I couldn't think clearly anymore. I did not want to have a mastectomy if it was not necessary, but I had begun to worry that we might never find a breast surgeon and plastic surgeon that would perform a lumpectomy on me. We had been told that we could take as long as two months before having to move forward with a surgery, but the cancer in my body felt like a ticking time bomb. I wanted it out. At that point, I didn't have the clarity of mind to make a decision about what to cook for dinner, let alone whether or not I should hold out and continue looking for another breast surgeon.

A few days later, I received a phone call regarding the scheduling of my surgery. I was advised that it would be necessary for me to arrive at the university at about 6 a.m., in order to have one final diagnostic test done. The hitch was, my surgery was not scheduled until four o'clock that afternoon.

"Let me get this straight. I have to be at the hospital by six o'clock in the morning for a diagnostic test but my surgery won't be until four o'clock. That's a ten hour wait. I just hang out for ten hours? I assume that during that time, I will not be allowed to eat or drink anything?" I imagined laying on a hospital gurney in some random hallway in a skimpy gown for ten hours. It also occurred to me that my surgery would take place very late on a Friday afternoon. I imagined they would release me within hours of my surgery, and I didn't like the thought that if anything went sideways, it might be difficult to track the doctor down on a Friday night.

There was no hesitation or hint of sympathy on the other end of the telephone line when the secretary replied, "Yes, that's correct. It is a ten hour wait, and you won't be able to eat or drink anything during that time."

"Can my husband stay with until the surgery?"

"No."

"Cancel my surgery."

At the end of the day, it turned out to be a really easy decision.

We pressed forward in our search for another breast surgeon. I prayed for Jesus to send me a sign to let me know when I had found the right breast surgeon, and He sent one, loud and clear.

On January 26th, 2012, Michael and I drove out to Hoag Hospital in Newport Beach. This is where the offices of Dr. Lincoln Snyder (real name) were located. When I walked up to sign in, I noticed a small business card holder sitting next to the sign in sheet. Inside this holder were "prayer cards." These small cards resembled those RSVP inserts that come along with a wedding invitation; they allowed you to write down your name and a request for a prayer. Have you ever in your life seen a stack of prayer cards in a physician's office? Me, neither. Obviously, his faith was more important to this doctor than being politically correct. I knew in that instant that I had found my doctor. My body, my cancer, was going to be turned over to a man who worshiped the Lord. It could not get any better than that. I filled out a prayer card, but I knew my prayers had already been answered.

My name was called and Michael and I were led into an exam room. By now, I knew the drill. I had shed any modesty about exposing my breasts. (To Michael's great embarrassment, after my surgery, I was willing to expose them at the drop of a dime. If, during a conversation with just about anyone, the topic of breast cancer came up, I would offer to expose my perky hooters.)

Dr. Snyder walked in. He reminded me of a grown up version of Ron Howard when he played the role of Opie on The Andy Griffith Show. He was tall and slender, with strawberry blonde hair that fell over one eye, and a spattering of freckles across the bridge of his nose. He had a sweet smile. In place of that snotty pretentiousness exhibited by the prior doctors we had seen, Dr. Snyder was actually soft spoken.

He introduced himself, shook our hands warmly, and wheeled a stool over to the side of the examining table. Already, the vibe felt very different in that room. Dr. Snyder began by going over my past medical history, patiently and thoroughly. If a question was posed that required a long, involved answer, Dr. Snyder sat back and let both Michael and I take our time sorting through our thoughts and responses. Sometimes, he added notes to my chart. This was not a doctor who was going to rush through anything. The three of us sat in that exam room for about an hour. After a brief exam, I was told that I could get dressed and we would meet with Dr. Snyder in his office down the hallway. Michael and I had already decided that this was the doctor we had been looking for. We were willing to take his advice, whatever it might be.

He was sitting behind his desk. I could see thumbnail images of my mammogram on the computer screen facing him. He glanced down at his notes, and back up at us.

"Melissa, I'm going to advise that you have a lumpectomy."

A loud buzzing sound began in my ears. I knew from past experiences this was a precursor to fainting. The buzzing drowned out the words that were being spoken. I sat perfectly still and stared at a poster hanging on the wall behind the doctor's desk. By outward appearances, I probably looked quite calm. In truth, my brain couldn't keep up with the rapid-fire questions I was asking myself. Had I heard correctly? Had the first two doctors been wrong, and we had been right? Were there actually breast cancer surgeons who were advising women to mutilate their bodies unnecessarily?

I remained in LaLa Land as Dr. Snyder painstakingly explained his strategy to us while illustrating my surgery on a Xeroxed copy of a woman's breast. I could feel Michael fidgeting next to me, and I knew the reason why. He was waiting for an opening in the conversation because he couldn't wait to ask the million-dollar question. The moment there was a pause in the conversation, he asked, "Statistically, what is the difference in mortality and recurrence rates if one compares a lumpectomy to a mastectomy with Melissa's specific cancer?" There was no hesitation in Dr. Snyder's answer. "The mortality rate and the rate of recurrence of cancer would be exactly the same, whether she had a mastectomy or a lumpectomy."

I sat in stunned silence as Michael began to bombard the doctor with questions. This is why it is so crucial to bring another person with you during any doctor appointments or diagnostic testing. You, the patient, can't expect yourself to ask the right questions, or retain any information. Your backup person should be the one to listen, to ask questions, to remember what the doctor said.

The questions and answers went back and forth between Michael and Dr. Snyder, but I had already shut down. It had been confirmed that I was a viable candidate for a lumpectomy, and that was the only thing I cared about. Forget about the diagnostic tests, the specialists that I would need to see, the lab work that needed to be done, or the specifics of the procedure for the lumpectomy. Michael, the scientist and guardian angel of my health, was immediately on top of the situation and had the wherewithal to ask all the right questions. By the time we left that office, we had our breast surgeon, plastic surgeon, and oncologist lined up. We had accomplished the daunting task of finding our perfect team.

It still haunts me that a woman diagnosed with breast cancer runs the risk of having an unnecessary mastectomy because her doctor doesn't want to bother with a complicated surgery. If Michael and I had not spent the time and energy doing research online and educating ourselves as much as we could about my cancer, I would now be missing one breast, maybe two. Please, please, do your homework.

A TRIP TO THE VET

Moral of the chapter: Having Faith

Faith played a fundamental role throughout my battles with cancer. I've always had a firm belief in Jesus Christ and over the years, my faith has deepened. Long before cancer, I tried to live my life in accordance with God's wishes, emphasis on *tried*. As a Christian, I sometimes stumble and fall, make mistakes, lose sight of what is important. I disappoint God. I never let those sins prevent me from turning back to my heavenly Father and praying for forgiveness. I always keep in mind how much I love my own sons, how that love is unconditional. I know my Creator loves me in the same way.

During my most desperate moments, the times when I thought cancer was going to take my life, I relied heavily on the following scripture.

Proverbs 3:5: Trust in the Lord with all your heart, and lean not on your own understanding.

I came to truly understand what *"lean not on your own understanding"* meant through a most unexpected source.

■■

My dad was never an animal lover. The few pets that we were able to smuggle into our house when I was a child didn't last very long. Just a few examples:

The first pet that I remember was Lucky, a little black kitty we found huddled under the shrubs in our yard. We brought her in and begged my mom, who had a much bigger heart than my old man, to let us keep her. Within a day, it became apparent that Lucky had dysentery. Cleaning up kitty diarrhea was a deal breaker for my mom, who had her hands full trying to take care of four kids. After a brief two day stay, Lucky went MIA. Our sweet beagle, Kimmy, vanished the day after she had been diagnosed with mange. Our guinea pig, Gus, disappeared the day after he bit my sister. The only pet my dad ever liked was a Boxer named Socks, so it's ironic that one afternoon Socks jumped the fence in our backyard and never came back.

My mom would tell us that these missing pets had decided they wanted to go to "a farm", where they could roam free and have plenty of friends. (We were told that Gus had gone to a "special zoo" to be with other guinea pigs.) We kids would cry for a few days, but since we never had a pet for an extended amount of time, we would get over it rather quickly.

As he aged, my dad softened up a lot. When he said he wanted to get a dog, my sister and I were ecstatic. (Not so much my mom, but we ignored her.)

On Father's Day, 2001, we took Dad to an animal shelter near his home. After going up and down each aisle, he returned to the kennel that held a small black and white puppy. The index card taped to the front of the cage read, "Australian Shepherd Mix. Male. Four months old."

Also in the kennel was a German shepherd puppy. His card read, "German Shepherd mix. Male. Four months." In much smaller print at the bottom of his card was this disclaimer: "Possible hip problem."

"Daddy, which dog are you looking at?"

"That little Aussie.

After lingering in front of the cage, I took charge over my dad's indecisiveness and tracked down an employee who was able to take the black and white puppy out of his kennel and into a small grass area located off the back of the building. The puppy stayed very still in the arms of the attendant as he was being carried into the yard. When the attendant placed him down on the grass, he stood there for a minute without moving. Finally, he hesitantly took a few steps forward. I thought his behavior was a little strange. After being locked up in that stinky kennel for so long, why wasn't this puppy leaping for joy at the fresh air, the sunshine, and the opportunity to be free?

"Why isn't he running around?"

"He's a little unsure about the grass. This little boy was born right here at the shelter. He doesn't get out very often. He's not used to standing on grass."

OMG. Just take a knife and stab me in the heart.

"Daddy, what do you think?"

"He's a good lookin' boy, that's for sure. But, I don't know, a puppy is a handful." He asked if the puppy was housebroken, and when the answer was no, I knew my dad wasn't going to take this dog. The thought of sending him back into the shelter made me sick to my stomach.

The attendant then shared this little tidbit. "Yeah, it's pretty sad. He had six littermates, and all of them have been rescued. Even the mom found a great home. But this little guy hasn't been so lucky. I really hope we don't have to put him down."

Well, I am only human.

"I'll take him."

My dad left empty handed that day, but I did not. I wrote a check for $50.00 and never looked back.

I can still vividly remember that two-hour drive home from Hemet to El Segundo. We found a small box, put a towel in the bottom of it, put the puppy in the box, and put the box on the backseat of my car. It was early evening when I headed home. The summer sunset was one of those breathtaking splashes of color across the sky that only a heavy layer of LA smog can produce. It was such a beautiful sight, I remember thinking, this is a sign that I made the right decision. I talked to the puppy the entire drive home, hoping my voice would be comforting to him. I told him he was going to have a wonderful life, full of doggie parks and walks and treats, and lots of love. I promised him I would always take good care of him and protect him, that he was going to have an awesome and long life. I watched him in my review mirror. He peered at me over the top of the box and seemed to be listening to every single word, but he didn't make a peep the entire drive home.

Did I mention that Michael hates dogs? As a child, he had a plethora of allergies, including cats and dogs. Also, he had a few bad experiences with dogs when he was a paperboy; as an adult he always seemed uncomfortable around dogs. In our fourteen years of marriage, I had tried on many occasions to persuade him that we needed a dog. We had raised four cats that had lived very long lives, found homes for three litters of kittens, and still had two adult cats with us. I don't know what made me take the leap that afternoon at the shelter. There was something so sad and soulful in this puppy's root beer colored eyes I guess my common sense took backseat to my heart.

I knew there would be resistance on Michael's part. I didn't expect a happy greeting when I walked into our house with a puppy that wasn't even housebroken. Still, somewhere deep inside I knew I made the right decision.

Michael's reaction was pretty much what I had expected. I walked through our front door and set the box down on our dining room floor, happily exclaiming, "Happy Father's Day!" This was probably the worst line I could have used. It would have been like Michael handing me a membership to a gym as an anniversary present. He glared into the box and snapped, "What in the hell is that?"

"It's a puppy!"

"Take it back."

"Honey, I can't take it back!"

"Have you lost your mind?"

I started to cry.

"Honey, please, just give him a chance. He was born at the animal shelter—born there! And he had six littermates and they all found homes, even the mommy, but this little boy was still there! He hardly knows what grass is because he's cooped up in a kennel all day….plus, he's four months old now and I don't know how long they keep puppies but they don't keep them forever! They put them down!"

I lifted the puppy out of the box so Michael could get a good look.

"Look how beautiful he is! Look at those eyes!"

Michael stared at the little black and white bundle in my arms. The puppy stayed perfectly still but kept his soulful, sad eyes on Michael. It was working.

"Well, yeah, he's a really cute dog. What is he?"

"He's an Australian shepherd mix."

"Copper, Grey and Onyx are going to be really pissed about this. It's unfair to expect three adult cats to suddenly have a dog in their house."

"Look, this dog only weighs eight pounds. Grey, Onyx and Copper weigh about eighteen pounds. They're much bigger than the dog. They'll let him know who's in charge around here. And since the puppy is so young, he'll grow up thinking that cats aren't prey. He'll think it's normal to hang out with cats."

Michael was processing this information.

"Look, honey. I know you're a cat person. We've had more than our share of cats. I've always wanted a dog. I know it was really bad form to just bring this dog home unexpectedly, but when I saw him, something told me that this dog was meant to be ours."

"Hmmmm."

Then he asked the question I had been dreading most. "Is he housebroken?"

I knew I had to go on the defensive right away.

"Is he *housebroken*? I just rescued this puppy from an animal shelter. Do you really think they housebreak the dogs at a shelter? Do you think they take them for daily walks, too? Newsflash; they don't. The dogs in the shelter are lucky if they even get out of their cages for a few minutes a day!" I wanted Michael to visualize the miserable conditions that went with being in an animal shelter.

"And while we're on the subject, he probably needs to go potty right now." I stepped out onto the deck and put the puppy down. He sniffed around for a minute and then did something that made a huge impact on Michael's decision. (*If you have a weak stomach—skip the following paragraph!*)

The little puppy did a little poop. We watched in horror as he turned around and began to eat the poop. I know, I'm sorry-this is so disgusting-but this behavior decided the puppy's fate.

I rushed over and moved him to another part of the deck. Michael, the man with a stomach of steel, began to gag. When he was able to compose himself he asked, "What in the hell was that?"

"That was what dogs in an animal shelter learn to do. They want to keep their cages clean; I'm sure most shelters don't have enough staff to check for dog poop in every kennel 24/7. So if it's not picked up right away, the dog eats it." That's when I leaned over the railing and barfed.

Michael might not have been a dog lover, but any misery of any animal truly disturbed him. He walked over to the puppy and reached down to pat his head.

"Hey, buddy."

"Buddy! That's a great name! Let's name him Buddy!" And so we did.

The cats adjusted with amazing ease.

I began doing research on crate training, housebreaking, a healthy diet, and socializing a dog. One of the things I learned was that it was important to familiarize yourself with your puppy's body. You're supposed to run your hands over your dog every day, checking for lumps or wounds or anything out of the ordinary. The first time I rolled Buddy on his back so that I could check his smooth pink tummy, I thought I detected a small lump on the left side of his abdomen. I waited a few hours, and checked again. That time, I didn't feel the lump. Over the next week, I kept checking his tummy, and the lump would come and go. Sometimes, I could feel it and even see a little bulge, other times, nothing.

I had also noticed that when I walked Buddy, he didn't seem to have enough stamina to walk more than a block. After that distance, he would just sit down. No matter how hard I yanked on his leash, he refused to get up, so I would have to carry him the rest of the way home. He also hated stairs, so when I was housebreaking him, I had to carry him up and down the stairs that led to our backyard.

These small imperfections were greatly outweighed by the positive aspects of our new family member. Buddy was a very gentle dog that was friendly to people, dogs and cats. He loved to chase squirrels, but every time he caught up with one, he would stand still with his nose a few inches away from the terrified little rodent, and then turn and run away. (I kept waiting for the time when a squirrel would drop dead from a heart attack.) The hunter-killer instincts that he had inherited from his ancestors, the wolf, were triggered by anything that moved quickly. He loved the chase. But the killer instinct must have been domesticated out of him over the generations. His only natural enemy seemed to be crows, and that was fine with me because I think the only good crow is a dead crow.

I had great success with obedience training, not because I had any special talent for that, but because Buddy was so intelligent. One evening after another, Michael would come home from work and Buddy and I would show off the new behavior he had mastered that day.

One brief month had passed before the first of many traumas befell Buddy. I was checking his tummy one afternoon, and I could clearly see and feel a lump. This time, it was undeniable. I immediately took him to the vet, who drew some blood and palpated on Buddy's abdomen. He couldn't feel or see anything. I told him the lump seemed to come and go, but that there was definitely a lump. I was beginning to worry that the vet was going to think I was being a hypochondriac for my dog, like I had Munchausen syndrome-by proxy disease. Possibly just to appease me, he offered to take an X ray. I could visualize the credit card bill that I was racking up-but in this situation I didn't feel like I could take any chances.

When he returned to the exam room carrying my puppy and the X-ray films, the vet looked downright sheepish. He cleared his throat and then said, "Well, Melissa, you were right. There's a mass in Buddy's abdomen. I can't say for certain what it is; it could be cancer or a diseased kidney or any number of things. He needs further diagnostic tests to determine exactly what's going on. I'm going to suggest that you take him to the Animal Surgical and Emergency Center in West LA. I think it's the best facility of its kind in Southern California.

I just want to make sure that you understand how sick your puppy is. If you decide not to go forward with treatment, he's probably only going to last for about another week."

I was too busy sobbing to ask any questions. I picked Buddy up, paid his bill, and continued to cry all the way home. I was absolutely certain that Michael would say we were going to have to put the puppy down and I even understood that.

I decided that whatever time Buddy had left I would make really special. We drove through McDonalds on the way home from the vet and I bought him a cheeseburger. When we got home, I emptied his toy box and played with him on the floor for a very long time. I let him run around in our front yard unleashed, one of his favorite things to do. I thought about our drive home from the animal shelter, when I had made so many promises to this little black and white puppy. I was supposed to love and protect him, to give him a long and joyous life. Now, only four weeks later, his life was about to end.

Michael was on a business trip to Washington DC. By the time he called home that night, I was nearly hysterical. It took a few minutes for me to calm down and explain the situation. Michael's reaction was something I would never ever in my wildest dreams have predicted.

"This really pisses me off." (Yeah, I expected that. I thought he meant that the bad luck of rescuing a sick puppy really pissed him off.)

"This poor dog deserves a chance at life. He's been through enough already. I'll be home early tomorrow afternoon. Call the animal hospital and make an appointment for our boy."

To me, this loving attitude was nothing short of miraculous.

The California Animal Hospital in West Los Angeles is a state of the art facility. Dr. Phillip Gill, the surgeon we met with, is warm and patient and highly qualified. The first thing he pointed out was that Buddy was not an Australian shepherd mix-he was a smooth coat Border collie.

In order to better evaluate Buddy's condition, he ordered more X-rays and an ultrasound test. The results of those tests were devastating.

Dr. Gill returned to the exam room and told us that the ultrasound revealed Buddy had a hydro-nephritic left kidney and ureter. In layman's terms, that meant Buddy had been born with a diseased left kidney. That kidney had shut down and needed to be removed immediately. Michael asked what the prognosis would be if Buddy had the surgery. Dr. Gill was very optimistic about the outcome. It really came down to this; if Buddy didn't have the surgery he would die. If he had the surgery, he had an excellent chance at living a full life with only one kidney.

But wait, there's more.

Dr. Gill clipped the X rays of Buddy's lower abdomen over a light box. You didn't need to be a doctor to see that his hip bones were really messed up. His left hip was only slightly out of the socket, but the right hip socket and joint were horribly displaced.

Michael's reaction; "Holy shit."

"Folks, I hate to be the bearer of more bad news, but Buddy has severe hip dysplasia. The left hip might not require surgery, but that right hip is completely out of the socket. He's still growing, so the surgery has to be put off for about six months. But if he doesn't get that hip fixed, he's going to become severely arthritic, which is a very painful condition. Eventually, he'll lose mobility in that leg."

I flashed back to that afternoon at the animal shelter where I found Buddy. He had been sharing his kennel with a German shepherd puppy. At the bottom of the ID card for the German shepherd, someone had mistakenly written "possible hip problem." That information should have been written on Buddy's card.

Dr. Gill's suggestion was that we take this one step at a time. Do the kidney surgery, let the dog recover, and then worry about the hip surgery. We followed his advice, mostly because it was too overwhelming to think long-term at that point.

Let me just throw in here that Michael and I are not so wealthy that we look for ways to burn through our money. Shelling out these amounts of money was not something we did lightly.

We felt confident he would receive superior medical care at this facility so we signed the consent for surgery form. Dr. Gill took Buddy's leash, and our trusting little boy followed him without hesitation. I began to cry immediately.

This was early evening on a Thursday. Buddy's surgery would take place the following morning. If there were no complications, he would remain in the hospital under observation and on IV drips until Saturday afternoon.

Within one month, Buddy had been given two shots at life. Not only had he been rescued from the shelter, he had been rescued by a family that was willing to pay for a very expensive surgery.

I was crying because I knew it didn't seem that way to Buddy. He was living in the physical world, unable to see beyond his circumstances. His reality was that we had allowed him to be led away by a stranger that locked him up in a cage again. To him, by all outward appearances, he was back in an animal shelter, abandoned for a second time. I knew he would wake up from that surgery feeling pain for the first time in his life, and he would be alone. The same mommy and daddy, who had given him a home, had lavished him with love and provided a safe haven, were now the perpetrators of a world of misery. During his recuperation, he would be cooped up in a cage with IV's attached to his little body, and we would be nowhere in sight.

I considered staying at that hospital overnight, thinking that maybe Buddy would be able to smell my scent. But the facility was fairly large and there were many closed doors and long corridors between the surgery center, the recovery center, and the waiting room. It seemed highly unlikely that he might be able to pick up my scent. I begged to leave his special blanket with him, knowing that it smelled like home and might provide a little comfort. But the blanket was a source of contamination, and Buddy had to be kept in a sterile environment for the next two days, so I couldn't even do that.

The only way that we could save our beloved little puppy was to allow him to go through this traumatic experience.

When we were finally able to pick him up two days later, I held him close to me the entire drive home. He whimpered with joy and stayed in my arms long after we arrived home. His recuperation was speedy and thorough.

After the kidney debacle, we decided that Lucky should be Buddy's middle name. We were going to make sure that this dog, born with so much stacked against him, would have a long and wonderful life.

Six months later, Buddy made his second trip to Animal Surgical Center in order to have his hip fixed. Once again, I knew this experience would be terrifying for him. Far worse, he would perceive this as a second trip to hell, courtesy of mommy and daddy. He only understood the physical world, and could never understand that this experience was a blessing in disguise. The minute we walked through the doors into the surgery center, he began desperately trying to back out the door. Michael finally had to pick him up and carry him into an exam room. I, as usual, cried.

By the time we celebrated his first birthday, Buddy was a stunningly handsome sixty pound Border Collie that could out run and out jump most of the dogs at the dog park; he was the leader of the pack.

I was able to keep all of the promises that I had made to him on that summer afternoon in 2001. His life was full of trips to the dog park, evening walks, rides in the car, a box for his toys that was constantly replenished, and daily treats. Every night, before I got into bed, I would get down on the floor next to him and tell him a (very brief) good night story.

In early 2010, Buddy began to slip every time he attempted to cross the hardwood floor in our dining room. I had his toenails clipped, thinking that was the problem, but apparently that wasn't the problem. The slipping didn't improve. Buddy began to intermittently lose the strength in his hind legs. He would be walking, and suddenly his back legs would just fold underneath his body.

We took him to Dr. Gill, the surgeon who had removed Buddy's diseased kidney and fixed his deformed hip many years before. Tragically, this time there was no surgery that could save Buddy's life. He was diagnosed with spinal cord cancer.

His decline was very cruel and rapid. Within about one week, he had completely lost the ability to use his back legs. The only way he could get around was to fold his back legs underneath him and drag himself with his front legs. Often times, when his legs gave out suddenly, he would look over at me with an expression of confusion on his face, as if to ask. "Why don't my legs work anymore?" I could see the light in his soulful, beautiful brown eyes beginning to dim. He could no longer go to the park, or for a drive in the car; his only trips outside were when we carried him out to the front yard. Toward the very end, he started to exhibit a truly disturbing symptom. When I would lie down on the floor next to him, he refused to look at me. He would get up and drag himself away from me. I knew he was trying to tell me that it was time to let him go.

On March 16th, one month shy of his ninth birthday, we had a vet come to our home to euthanize Buddy. I laid down on the floor next to him, and right before the final med, when I knew he could still hear me, I promised him that I would find him in Heaven. He closed his beautiful eyes for the last time.

His work here was done.

Michael and I had come to the conclusion that although we had chosen Lucky as Buddy's middle name, we were the ones who had been lucky. The love and joy he brought to our family had been a precious gift.

One evening shortly after my cancer diagnosis, I began looking for scripture that would lift me up and give me strength. Proverbs 3:5 caught my attention. I read and reread it. The first half of the scripture, *"Trust in the Lord with all your heart"* was quite clear. I stopped to reflect on the second half of the scripture, *"Lean not on your own understanding."*

In all honesty, I cannot tell you what made my mind wander to thoughts of Buddy. We have a picture of him in our living room; maybe my eyes settled on that picture. It was always difficult to think about Buddy without remembering the trauma he had to endure during his first year with us. We never had a single doubt that he had loved us as much as we had loved him, but I'm sure his little puppy brain could not have comprehended why we had put him through such brutal experiences.

That was when I made the connection. We always loved Buddy. We always wanted the very best for him. The times that he had felt we had abandoned and betrayed him were actually the times that we were saving his life. But Buddy could only lean on his own understanding.

Now I understood Proverbs 3:5.

The harrowing or heartbreaking situations that we all endure throughout our lives are often not what they appear to be. Our heavenly Father has a plan and a reason for every aspect of our lives. We have to trust *with all our hearts* that He is not punishing or abandoning us. We have to look beyond our physical situation, and ask ourselves: what lessons were learned? Did something positive come out of the negative experience? Was the direction of your life changed? Could you become a source of guidance for others?

I believe were very definite reasons for my battles with cancer. Writing a book had always been a dream of mine, but as my life unfolded, the more it seemed that dream was unattainable. Who was I to think I had the talent or perseverance to write a book? Also, what could I possibly write about that would be so interesting or informative, people would want to read my book? When I became a three time cancer survivor, I knew I had to tell my story. So I wrote this book. My dream is now a reality

I don't think it was mere coincidence that I went to an animal shelter seeking a pet for my father and instead ended up bringing a dog home for myself. I believe that it was all part of God's plan that through a sick and unwanted puppy, I would learn the true meaning of faith.

Buddy Lucky Meshishnek

The following chapter serves to share with readers, information that I gathered while researching Melissa's cancers. The information herein should not be substituted for professional medical care or advice.

TRANSLATION, PLEASE

By Dr. Michael J. Meshishnek, Ph.D.

Moral of the Chapter: Understanding Diagnostic Tests

My purpose in writing this chapter is to demystify the diagnostic tests involved in breast cancer and to explain how to interpret test results.

I received my Ph.D. in organic chemistry from the University of California, Santa Barbara, in 1978. My background in chemistry proved to be an invaluable tool for deciphering the information on breast cancer that was available through the Internet.

I remember the day we went for Melissa's follow up mammogram. On more than one occasion, she had received a follow-up letter from the imaging center indicating that they wanted to do a repeat mammogram. She had never asked me to go with her when she had these tests done. I sensed that she was nervous about this follow-up test, probably because she hadn't had a mammogram in about three years. It was the first time I attended one of these appointments.

We went to the breast-imaging center and were relieved when Melissa's name was called so quickly. I'm not the type who reads magazines or checks my phone incessantly. I pull on my mustache, rub my chin, wring my hands, or tap my feet up and down. I fidget. I began to notice that women were coming and going. We had arrived at the facility at about 2:00. As the half-hours ticked by, I became quietly agitated. At about 4:30, I asked the receptionist to check on Melissa's status. The receptionist proceeded to get on the phone and then said, "We're very busy today and she's being taken care of right now." I sat down and waited. About 10 minutes later, Melissa appeared from a corridor that no one else had used. As she raced past m she blurted out: "I have breast cancer!"

My first thought was that Melissa had misunderstood something. This follow up mammogram was just a preliminary test, it was much too soon for anyone to have made that diagnosis.

"You have breast cancer? How can they possibly know that you have breast cancer this soon?"

"OK, they said they *think* I have breast cancer. But I saw the images and there were definitely some weird spots in my breast!"

"Who *thinks* you have breast cancer?"

"The head of Radiology!" Oh. Not good.

Once home, we tried to calmly discuss the situation. I kept insisting that this diagnosis was far too premature. It was my job to comfort and reassure my wife. I didn't want her to know that I was just as terrified as she, and with good reason.

I was nine years old when my mother had been diagnosed with breast cancer. Her suffering had been unbearably prolonged and relentless. Tragically, it probably could have been prevented.

When she had discovered a lump in her breast, she immediately made an appointment see her OB/GYN. That doctor told her it was a blocked milk gland, and that she should just keep an eye on it. The lump continued to grow. When it was about the size of a golf ball, she consulted with a highly recommended surgeon. I remember her coming home from the surgeon's appointment, entering through the front hallway sobbing, completely undone. She said, "The doctor says I have to have surgery and we won't know until we do surgery what the situation is." The doctor was extremely concerned and wanted to operate as soon as possible. A few days later, she was hospitalized and underwent a radical mastectomy. I remember her coming home from the hospital and bravely pulling back her blouse to show me a ton of elastic bandages covering the area where her breast had been. I gently touched the area, thinking some of her breast must still be underneath all those bandages. But it was all gone. I found out later that she had lymph node involvement, which was why they had performed a radical mastectomy. The surgeon had removed so much tissue my mom was just skin and rib bones on one side. It was a horrifying and pitiful sight.

At some time after the mastectomy, she had radiation. I don't remember how long she had to undergo treatment but I remember her showing me part of her chest plate. Her skin was blistered and an angry red color, it hurt just to look at it. The strategy after radiation was that the surgeon would watch my mother closely for five years. The presumption was after five years, she would be okay and out of the danger zone.

After about four and one-half years, a follow up x-ray showed spots on her lungs about the size of a match head. My family began to quietly freak out, each member in their own private way. The surgeon told us he would recheck my mom again in six months. Six months later, the spots were more distinct and visible.

In an effort to prevent further growth of these spots, my mom underwent surgery to have her ovaries and adrenal glands removed. The surgery, where they cut her belly from one end to the other, immediately threw her into menopause, which made her despondent and glum. If that weren't bad enough, they had given her hormone therapy, which essentially consisted of testosterone injections in an attempt to reverse the growth of the spots. The thinking was that many breast cancers are "estrogen positive" and feed off estrogen produced by the body. Nowadays, the protocol is to try to prevent the body from making estrogen. My mother was miserable. In the end, the cancer metastasized and spread throughout her body.

Her esophagus had been so badly damaged by the x-ray radiation exposure that she had trouble eating even the smallest amount of food. She would vomit after every meal. She was 4'11" and when healthy weighed about 120 pounds. Her weight dropped to a skeletal 85 pounds. She passed away the day before my 19th birthday. She was 44 years old.

When I compare what my mother went through and what Melissa went through, the treatment for cancer seemed fundamentally the same; the cancer is cut out (surgery) and then burned out (radiation.) Along the way, some poison (chemotherapy) and hormone therapy are thrown into the mix.

However, the surgical and diagnostic techniques have made quantum leaps. The radiation therapy protocols are much more exacting, much more precise and controlled than they were in the sixties. The chemotherapeutic agents that they use now are far superior to what was used then. Great strides have been made through breast cancer research, but what hasn't changed is the toll this formidable disease exacts on its victims.

BREAKING DOWN DIAGNOSTIC TESTS

MAMMOGRAM:

The mammogram is a standard test that looks for different types of tissue in the breast using x-rays. It's basically an x-ray of the breast. In this test, breast tissue looks grey but anything that is more dense than the normal breast tissue appears lighter, more white. Very similar to an x-ray of bone. Bone is white, fractures are grey. Dark spots or changes in grey to white are a red flag on a mammogram. A follow up mammogram would be ordered for the patient.

ULTRASOUND TEST:

This test uses very high-pitched sound waves known as ultrasonic sound, which probe the tissue by measuring the reflection of the sound off the tissue. This can be done in real time, unlike an x-ray or mammogram, which is a one-shot deal. A wand is held against the breast, the area covered with gel or fluid to help transmit or couple the sound into the tissue. Reflected sound will vary in intensity depending on the density of the tissue. Generally speaking, the ultrasound is much more definitive than the mammogram and will usually give an indication of the size and location of some unusual growth. Since this is a real-time technique it is often used in conjunction with a needle biopsy.

ULTRASOUND GUIDED NEEDLE BIOPSY:

An ultrasound guided needle biopsy uses the picture generated in real time from the ultrasound to guide the needle to the area of concern, i.e. a tumor. The tissue sample is obtained by extracting some of the tissue in the area of concern with a needle. This tissue sample is sent to a pathologist who will examine it microscopically to determine whether the tissue is benign or cancerous.

According to the structure of the cells, the pathologist assigns a grade to the tissue. Breast cancer is normally graded from a scale of one to three. This grade is a score that tells you how different the cancer cells appearance and growth patterns are from those of normal healthy breast tissue.

> *Grade 1*, or low-grade cancer cells look similar to or a little bit different from normal cells. These tend to grow in slow well-organized patterns. Generally speaking grade 1 cells do not divide very rapidly to make new cancer cells. Grade 1 cells are sometimes also called well-differentiated cells.

> *Grade 2*, or intermediate grade cancer cells do not look like normal cells and appear to be growing and dividing a little faster than normal tissue. Grade 2 cells are often referred to as moderately-differentiated cells.

> *Grade 3*, or high-grade cancer cells look very different from normal cells. They appear to be growing quickly and in disorganized, irregular patterns with many of them dividing quickly to make new cancer cells. Grade 3 cells are referred to as poorly-differentiated cells.

Tumor grades are determined by the results of the biopsy and pathology report. A low grade, or grade 1 cancer can be encouraging since it is growing slowly but also might be tougher to kill or treat because it is growing slowly. On the other hand, having a high-grade cancer is of concern because of the rapid growth rate. However, conversely, keep in mind that these high-grade cancers are easier to kill because they are more vulnerable to drugs and radiation due to their rapid cellular division.

STAGING OF CANCER:

The stage of the cancer essentially refers to the size of the tumor and how much it has grown. For breast cancer, there are basically two types of cancer.

Ductal Carcinoma: *in situ*

> Ductal Carcinoma *in situ* or, DCIS, is essentially stage zero cancer. The cancer cells in the breast are still contained in the milk ducts, and have not spread to the outside duct walls.

Ductal Carcinoma: *ex situ*

> Ductal Carcinoma *ex situ,* is cancer that has grown beyond the milk ducts walls. This is classified as Stage 1 cancer.

Stage I

Stage I cancer is a very early breast cancer with the size of the tumor less than 2 centimeters (2.5 centimeters =1 inch). Stage I cancer also means there is no cancer present in the lymph nodes.

Stage II

When a cancer tumor grows beyond 2 centimeters, it becomes stage II. There are differentiations of stage II cancer, depending on whether there is lymph node involvement or not.

Stage III

When the tumor is 5 centimeters in size it becomes stage III. Stage III cancer usually has lymph node involvement.

Stage IV

When the tumor is larger than 5 centimeters, or has spread to other parts of the body it is known as stage IV.

There is no stage V.

In addition to grade and stage, there are other factors that influence treatment of breast cancer. In order of importance, they are:

-The size, or stage of the cancer.

-Lymph node involvement.

-Oncotype, or oncology type.

The Oncotype score is derived from genetic testing of the tumor sample. Samples of the diseased tissue that have been removed during breast surgery are sent to a laboratory, where they are compared to approximately two-dozen different genes in our cells. Although results from Onco scores can be graded on a scale of 1-100, it is more common for the chart on which the results are plotted to include only 1-50. I am not a medical doctor but my guess is that it is extremely rare to have an Oncotype score higher than 50. The higher the Oncotype score is, the nastier the cancer. More aggressive treatments will be required to cure the patient.

If you or someone you love has a high Oncotype score, take heart in this: Melissa's Oncotype score was 42.

Other Factors That Influence A Cancer Diagnosis:

Breast cancer is either estrogen positive and/or progesterone positive. Estrogen positive cancer means that the cancer feeds on Estrogen. Progesterone cancer means that the cancer feeds on progesterone.

The HER2 factor will also be a consideration in the treatments for the cancer. HER2 positive cancers tend to grow faster and are more likely to spread and re-occur relative to HER2 negative types.

The last factor is the KI–67, which is another growth factor. A high KI-67 factor translates to a more aggressive cancer that rapidly grows and divides. A high KI-67 means that the tumor is a nasty one, but as I wrote earlier, there is a positive side to that diagnosis. These tumors have a great track record of responding extremely well to certain treatments. That means medical science has figured out how to kill those damn cells.

MRI (MAGNETIC RESONANCE IMAGING):

If a needle biopsy confirms cancer, an MRI test will follow. Magnetic resonance imaging or MRI images tissue by looking at how it responds to a strong magnetic field when radio-frequency radiation is applied. Using a very elaborate computerized facility, one can get clear images of tissues to easily discern one type of tissue from another. Since most tissue is basically magnetic at the atomic level, this allows the MRI technique to image tissues by flipping their magnetic nuclei in a radio field and detecting the signal. Normal tissue and cancerous tissues respond differently to these radio signals.

An MRI is really the best technique for finding cancerous tumors, sizing them, and allowing placement of wires and markers for the surgeon to use as boundaries during his excision.

Just as an aside, I was able to stand next to Melissa to hold her hand throughout this test. Due to a traumatic childhood incident, she is extremely claustrophobic, so this test is a very difficult one for her. In order to place herself in the required position for the test, she had to kneel on all fours until her breasts were hanging directly over two holes that were cut out in the table. Most women would have found kneeling on a table on all fours with her breasts swinging to and fro, a humiliating experiencing. Melissa was laughing hysterically. Then again, that might be attributed to the two Valium she had ingested before the test.

In our experience, each time another diagnostic test was done, the calculated size of the suspected tumor increased. The mammogram showed a spot the size of a tiny green pea. The more sensitive ultrasound revealed an area about the size of a navy bean. By the time we got to the MRI, the affected site was allegedly nearly 7 centimeters. However, post surgery, the pathology report on the actual tumor was 2.1 centimeters, essentially right on the border between stage I and stage II. For patients recently diagnosed with breast cancer, keep this in mind; the equipment being used for diagnosis is so sensitive it may actually enlarge or magnify the image of the cancer.

STEREOTACTIC NEEDLE BIOPSY:

The final diagnostic test a patient will undergo is a stereotactic needle biopsy, which is generally done a few hours prior to surgery. This test uses two-dimensional x-rays to image the area of suspicion. During this procedure, very thin wire markers are inserted into the breast. These wires are used as indicators, allowing the surgeon to know exactly where the cancer is and how much tissue needs to be removed to guarantee clean margins. This procedure has a very bizarre twist to it. The wires that have been inserted deep into the breast tissue extend about four inches out of the side of the breast. The technician called them "cat whiskers," which was a very apt description of what they resembled. During her lumpectomy, Dr. Snyder was going to check Melissa's healthy breast because one of the diagnostic tests had revealed a small dark spot, and he wanted to make certain that the spot was only benign calcifications. That meant both of her breasts had to have wires inserted into them. The cat whiskers not only looked totally weird, they immediately became a source of pain. If Melissa let her upper arms brush against the wires, they would poke sharply into her skin.

Once all of your diagnostic tests are complete, you and your breast surgeon will have to decide which procedure is the right procedure for you.

LUMPECTOMY:

This is a breast conserving procedure. Only the cancerous tissue and a small amount of healthy tissue to ensure healthy margins are removed. The nipples are preserved, but the surgery usually causes nerve damage to that area. Typically, there is no sensation to the nipples after the surgery.

Once the lumpectomy is completed, a plastic surgeon will immediately do reconstructive surgery on the healthy breast, so that the patient's breasts are a matched set.

MASTECTOMY:

This is a procedure where the entire breast is removed. The woman who requires a mastectomy has some decisions to make regarding reconstructive surgery following the removal of her breast.

RADIATION THERAPY:

Radiation therapy for breast cancer consists of a very controlled series of short exposures to x-rays on the affected surgical area. It is usually a quick 2-minute zap. Melissa underwent radiation from Monday through Friday for six weeks. Radiation therapy kills even microscopic bits of cells of cancer that were not removed during the surgery.

CHEMOTHERAPY:

Chemotherapy is generally used to treat patients with cancer that has spread from the original tumor site to other areas in the body, a process known as metastasis. Chemotherapy is designed to destroy cancer cells anywhere in the body.

You perhaps can begin to see how these treatments work together to cover all the bases. A good clean surgical excision with good margins gets essentially the whole tumor. If there are other little bits and pieces in the general area, radiation therapy burns them out. If any cells have broken loose and traveled around the body through the blood stream or lymphatic system, chemotherapy wipes them out. When a cancer has been removed by surgery, chemotherapy can be used to prevent the cancer from coming back.

There are more than 50 different types of chemotherapy drugs available to treat cancer, with even more being tested. Your oncologist chooses the drug or combinations of drugs that will be most beneficial to your specific cancer.

Chemotherapy works by killing cells in the bloodstream and lymphatic system and any part of the body that is fed by these. Chemotherapy drugs interfere with the ability of these fast growing cells to grow, divide and multiply. Unfortunately, there are other types of cells in the body that grow rapidly too, such as bone marrow (that produce blood cells), cells in the stomach and the intestines. Also, hair follicles are rapidly growing cells that are targeted by chemo, which is why chemo patients lose their hair at some point during treatment.

In many cases, chemotherapy medicines are given in combination, which means you get two or three different medicines at the same time. These combinations are known as chemotherapy regimens. In early stage breast cancer, standard chemotherapy regimens lower the risk of the cancer coming back. In advanced breast cancer, chemotherapy regimens make the cancer shrink or disappear in about 30-60% of people treated. Keep in mind that every cancer responds differently to chemotherapy.

Chemotherapy drugs are administered in various ways depending on the drugs given and the cancer type. These can include oral, injection, through a catheter port, or even topically. For breast cancer, generally the drugs are administered intravenously by injection into a vein from an IV bag over a period of hours. In Melissa's case, her regimen consisted of Taxotere and Cytoxane, along with anti-nausea medications, steroids and anti-anxiety meds.

Side Effects

Unfortunately, along with the chemo drugs come some really bad side effects. It is important to understand that these can be managed fairly well by your Oncologist and his team. Not everyone has the same set of side effects. Typical adverse side effects are:

Nausea and vomiting

Loss of appetite

Taste blindness or changes in food taste

Hair loss

Anemia and fatigue

Diarrhea

Infection

Easy bleeding or bruising

Sores in the mouth and throat

Neuropathy and other nervous system damage

Kidney damage

Blurred vision

Most of these side effects can be partially controlled with the addition of extra medications along with your chemo infusion. These medications are designed to control nausea:

Decadron

Zantac

Benadryl

Zofran

Ativan

Aloxi

Emend

These, too, have adverse side effects. Attempts to control nausea may bring other unwanted side effects like diarrhea and headaches.

Steroids can also be part of a chemo regimen. For Melissa, steroids were both a curse and a blessing. They gave her a boost of desperately needed energy and were crucial in helping strengthen her immune system. They also made her hot, sweaty, and bitchy. I remember driving home after one of her sessions, and she looked over at me and said, "I feel grrrreat! Like Tony the Tiger!" Her eyes were unusually wide, and she seemed unable to sit still. She kept fiddling with the radio, the glove compartment, her visor, and her side view mirror. It was typical for Melissa to be quiet, sometimes even nod off, during the hour it took us to drive home after her chemo treatments. On this afternoon, she didn't shut up the entire drive home. That's steroids for you.

BLOOD COUNTS:

It is important to understand that the chemo drugs and the other medications wreak havoc on your blood chemistry. When you undergo chemo treatments, two things are certain. First, they will weigh you before every treatment because your treatment dosage is based on your weight. Also before every treatment, they will take a blood sample and do a workup to determine your red blood count, white blood count, and platelet count. They also check for minerals like sodium, calcium and potassium. Chemo drugs destroy many of your blood cells so it is important to monitor the red blood count to prevent anemia. The white blood count may also plummet, and this increases the risk of infection. Similarly, if the platelets in the blood get destroyed, the patient will experience bruising or bleeding.

There are ways to control how great a toll chemo will take on a patient's blood. First of all, the white blood cells can be rapidly replenished with a white blood cell booster drug such as Neulasta. It is commonly given the day after chemo treatment via intra-muscular injection. It works by stimulating the growth of neutrophils, which are a type of infection fighting white blood cells. The Neulasta signals the bone marrow to make more neutrophils. If the patients red blood count gets too low they might be given an infusion of iron which will help the body produce more red blood cells. Platelets are a problem in that only a transfusion can restore them. So you kind of have to tough this one out.

HYDRATION THERAPY:

Hydration therapy is another IV treatment using primarily saline solution with a few of the above-mentioned meds. Sometimes minerals are added too, if you have become deficient in any, such as calcium. The purpose of hydration therapy is essentially to flush out all of the toxins produced by the chemo treatment. Imagine it like this: you spray pesticide around your house to kill ants, roaches, or termites. The insects die, but you still have to sweep up the dead carcasses. Hydration therapy flushes out many of the dead cells and reaction products of the chemo agents with cells. Getting rid of these toxins makes you feel a lot better. Sometimes hydration treatments every other day are required for the first week after chemo. Often the addition of a steroid and/or Benadryl will also give the patient tremendous relief. The benefits of hydration therapy for Melissa were phenomenal.

Chemo treatments (for breast cancer patients) are usually staged at three-week intervals. You get the chemo treatment on a Monday, then return the next day for a Neulasta shot (white blood cell booster), and then return as you see fit for hydration therapy. Generally the next Monday they check your blood. After 21 days the treatment is repeated. Usually 4-6 treatments are required.

HORMONE THERAPY:

Hormone therapy is a type of chemotherapy. Very often, the cancer cells or tumor, are of the Estrogen/Progesterone positive type and feed on these hormones like sugar. There are drugs that can inhibit or prevent the cancer from eating or receiving estrogen. One drug, Tamoxifen, binds to the tumor receptors that eat the estrogen-so hopefully these cells eventually die. For women who still have active ovaries and are producing estrogen, this is the drug of choice. However, hormone therapy can have side effects such as body aches and hot flashes.

For women who have passed menopause or have had their ovaries removed, other drugs are also available to block estrogen production in the body. Two of these are Arimidex and Aromasin. They work by blocking an enzyme path that converts other chemicals in the body into estrogen. No estrogen: no cell growth from this food source. These too, have side effects. You may have to try all of them to see which one works best for you. Hormone therapy is generally recommended for 10 years after all of your other treatments (surgery, radiation and chemo) are finished.

Michael's Top Ten Tips:

1. Request a copy of all test results. Place this paperwork in a notebook or file folder. Bring this folder with you to all of your doctor appointments.

2. Bring your spouse or a close friend/family member to all doctor visits and tests.

3. Do not hesitate to ask questions. If you don't understand the answer, ask again.

4. Make sure you have complete faith in your entire team of physicians. If you are unable to find a team close to home, research neighboring counties.

5. Get more than one opinion.

6. Make sure you understand exactly what is covered in your insurance policy. The journey that lays ahead is not only scary, it's really expensive. At the time Melissa was under treatment, the fee for one round of chemotherapy was $10,000.00.

7. Request hydration therapy with chemo. This is a lifesaver.

8. If you are able to, request that your oncologist give you a white blood cell booster the day after a chemo treatment. This boosts your white blood cell production and helps to prevent from getting infections.

9. You can't have too much imaging; more is better. You want your team to gather as much information possible about your cancer before you are on the operating table.

10. If your loved ones offer to help, let them help.

ARE MY NIPPLES SLIPPING?

Moral of the chapter: It looks worse than it feels

My breast surgery lasted for almost five hours. When I woke up in the recovery room, the first thing I saw was Michael standing next to the bed. He was holding my hand and smiling down at me. He leaned over and whispered, "Hi Mel! Everything went great. Dr. Snyder got good clean margins, and there was no lymph node involvement. You're going to be fine."

I've always had a high tolerance to medications. The other patients who were parked next to me in the room were still in a semi-comatose state after their surgeries. But I was already awake and clearheaded enough to understand those wonderful words.

"No lymph node involvement?" My greatest concern was that the cancer had spread.

"None." Although he looked tired and pale, he also looked really relieved. In my head, I began chanting praises of thanks to God.

There was a large clock on the wall across from me. I began to watch the hands tick the time away. One by one, the patients surrounding me were wheeled out of the recovery room until I was the last body still laying on a cold steel gurney. A nurse came in at some point, and turned off three of the four banks of overhead lights in the room. By now it was about 5 o'clock in the evening and I was starving. For some reason I had an overwhelming craving for a burrito, which was pretty weird because Mexican food isn't even one of my favorites.

A nurse would wander in every now and then for a brief drive by, checking my vital signs and disappearing through the door. I started to tell her I was starving and wanted a burrito, which always elicited a laugh. A young technician sat behind a desk across the room. Apparently, it was his job to stay in the room until all the patients were gone. As the evening dragged on, the young man became openly restless and agitated. He finally picked up the telephone and punched in one number after another, making inquiries as to why I was still hanging out in the recovery room.

By then I had reached the point where the good drugs were wearing off and the discomfort level was rising. I began whining and begging Michael to find out why I was still in the recovery room. He left the room, and returned a few minutes later to tell me that they were waiting for a bed to become available. Well, that was weird. I was in Dr. Snyder's office when his nurse arranged my hospital stay.

I was finally wheeled to my room, and introduced to the nurses that would be taking care of me. They were all very sweet and kind, but they looked so young to me. They helped me settle into my bed, got me hooked up to all the necessary IV's, checked my vital signs, and gave me a push of some kind of painkiller. I was beginning to slip away as one of the nurses put the blood pressure cuff on my arm. She pumped it up, looked at the reading, and then said, "Hmmmm… That can't be right." She took my blood pressure again, looked at the reading, and said, "Oh my God!" She threw the sphygmomanometer down on the bed, bolted from the room, and as she was running down the corridor I could hear her yelling for a doctor.

That jolted me back into consciousness. I listened to hear if a code blue to my room was broadcast over the P.A. system. (A code blue is the term used by hospitals to announce that a patient has gone into cardiac arrest. This code alerts a team of doctors to sprint to the appropriate hospital room with a crash cart.) Michael had been sitting over in the corner of the room on a pull out couch. He jumped up and came over to the side of the bed. "What's the matter?"

"I don't know! The nurse took my blood pressure and then freaked out!" I had experienced adverse side effects from anesthesia before, but nothing that ever involved my heart. This was terrifying! I could just picture those paddles they use to jump-start your heart being slapped over my freshly stitched breasts. Ouchhhh.

The nurse returned to the room, not with a physician, but with another, slightly older, nurse. That nurse took my blood pressure, and told me that it was way too low. I was asked to sit up and start wriggling around. I wanted to comply, but that painkiller push was kicking in. I tried a few lackluster moves, and then laid my head back down on the pillow. I think the terror of seeing the nurse's reaction to my blood pressure must have caused my body to release some adrenaline. My blood pressure increased a few numbers but it was still dangerously low. Michael told me that the nurses came in constantly for a few hours, telling me to sit up and move around. I guess I complied, but I don't remember any of this. Good drugs.

My sweet husband had endured a long night of trying to get a little sleep on a roll out bed that looked about as comfortable as a prison mattress. Not surprisingly, he looked more wiped out than me the following morning. Wouldn't it be great if our loved ones, the ones who stay at our side for hours on end, who don't get anything to eat, who get the most uncomfortable sleeping arrangement, would be offered a mild sedative as a night cap? Just a thought.

Dr. Snyder came in mid-morning to check things out before he checked me out. I wasn't sure if I wanted to look when he unwrapped the bandages, but my morbid curiosity forced me to look down at my chest when it was exposed. I can tell you this; it looked much worse than it felt. I've had stitches before, and I've always asked how many were necessary. I didn't bother to ask Dr. Snyder how many stitches he had to use, because the number would have been very disturbing to a hypochondriac like me.

There was a neat line of stitches underneath each breast that were in the shape of a happy face smile. Running around both of my nipples were more stitches. If I squinted my eyes to blur the stitches and dried blood, I could see the outline of my new breasts, and they were beauties! I later learned that Dr. Lawton, my plastic surgeon, had removed three pounds of breast tissue, an amount that seemed to have shocked even her. I'm happy to report that I came out of that operating room with absolutely perky hooters. My first thought was, *wow, my boobs haven't looked this good since high school.* But on second inspection, I realized my boobs looked *better* than they did in high school! Thank you again, Jesus!

Dr. Lawton also checked on me before I was discharged from the hospital. She thought everything looked great; I was fine to go home. The only warning we received was that if I developed a fever of 101 or higher, I was to return to the hospital immediately.

We had been home for a few hours when I began to feel warm. Michael took my temperature. It was 99 degrees. We waited a few minutes. My symptoms escalated into feeling feverish and achy. My next reading was 100 degrees. It was 7:00 on a Saturday night. The drive back to Hoag Hospital would take over an hour. The emergency room would be a hotbed of contagious bacteria and viruses. At my third reading, my temperature hit 101 degrees. "Honey, you need to call Dr. Lawton."

I could see Michael's hands shaking as he dialed Dr. Lawton's number. From what I could hear of his side of the conversation, nothing sounded urgent. Dr. Lawton's advice had been for me to take two Tylenol. If that didn't bring the fever down, we would have to drive back to the hospital. I took the Tylenol, and my temperature fell immediately. Michael and I climbed into bed and slept soundly for twelve hours.

Over the next few days, I would take one Vicodin every six hours, and can say in all honesty, the pain from my surgery was minimal. The real source of pain and agitation came from the drainage tubes that had been inserted into the side of both breasts and the middle of my right armpit. The purpose of these tubes was to draw out of my body any residual fluid that might accumulate in my breasts or my armpit (where lymph nodes had been removed) post –surgery. An oblong shaped bulb at the end of each tube caught the fluid that slowly seeped out of the wounds. Before I was discharged from the hospital, we (by that I mean, Michael) had been taught how to maintain the drainage tubes.

Just the sight of the pale pink liquid in the bottom of those bulbs made me lightheaded. I had been a brave little soldier thus far, but I just couldn't handle dealing with the drainage tubes. Thank God my husband has a stomach of steel. He gamely took over the revolting task of cleaning and emptying my tubes twice a day. In his best organic chemist voice, he would give me a blow-by-blow narrative of what he was doing. Knowing what a weak stomach I have, every now and then he would remark on what he had just thrown down the sink, and it would send me into a fit of gagging. Kind of a sick sense of humor, right?

Throughout my recovery period, I would pull my pajama top up every few hours to make sure my nipples had not slipped. I don't know why I feared that they would-they were stitched in very tightly.

For the first few days after surgery, I was supposed to leave a t-shirt on when I took a shower. This was to protect my stitches from the spray of water. On about day three, I began to experience a terrible burning and itching pain in my right armpit. I could tell that the pain was not related to the drainage tube, this was a new and different pain. The lymph node removal had restricted the range of motion in my arm. I asked Michael to help me remove my top, and I held a mirror under my armpit. I could see that the entire area was covered in a bright red rash, and was oozing clear fluid the way a blister does. Michael called Dr. Lawton, and she recognized the symptom immediately. "Oh, yes. That's very common. Melissa has a yeast infection." Michael looked puzzled. Believing she must have missed the part in their conversation when he said the rash was under my armpit, he repeated, "Dr. Lawton, this rash is under her armpit." Well, doesn't everyone associate a yeast infection with a hoo hoo? "I understand that. Melissa got a yeast infection because she must not have let her armpit dry out completely after her showers. Yeast can grow anywhere where it's warm and moist." Tubes dangling from my body, stitches everywhere, and a yeast infection under my armpit. I feel pretty.

Two weeks after my surgery, I had my post-operative office visit with Dr. Snyder. He had received the pathology reports taken during my surgery. Overall, the news was very good. It had been confirmed that all three sentinel lymph nodes that had been removed were free of cancer cells. The exact measurement of my tumor had been 2.1 centimeters, which was smaller than had been predicted by diagnostic tests. My tumor was a grade 3 and my DCIS (ductal carcinoma in situ) grade was "high". It was my Oncotype DX score that was cause for alarm. Onco scores are usually rated on a scale from one to fifty, one being excellent, fifty being the worst it can be. My score was 42. If the only therapeutic path I took after surgery was an oral hormone blocker, I ran an extremely high risk of recurrence. If I added chemotherapy and radiation to the regimen, it lowered my risk to a seven per cent chance. That was a no brainer.

'ROID RAGE

Moral of the chapter: Lesser Known Side Effects of Chemo

Walking into a chemo facility is like walking into a church. Everything is hushed, and everyone looks peaceful. Everyone looks peaceful because they are zoned out on whatever drug is being pumped into their cancer-ridden bodies. Some patients are sleeping, some are reading a book, and some are just lying there with that thousand-yard stare. There is always one patient who looks absolutely healthy, practically glowing, wearing a spiffy hat or scarf around her head. You would not have known she was sick, except for the catheter port attached to her chest.

Dr. Greg Angstreich, my oncologist, had been honest in letting me know that chemotherapy was not an exact science. There are standard protocols and medications used, but reactions to the meds vary from patient to patient. In the beginning, it's trial and error; first round, see how things go, second round, make any necessary adjustments. Repeat. Your oncologist is like a bartender. He mixes a cocktail until he founds the one that works best for you.

I was dreading my first round of chemotherapy, but it wasn't bad at all. The only part that was hard for me was getting the IV inserted into my arm.

Nurses and lab technicians have always told me that I have "bad veins." If I'm having blood drawn, it's never just one poke into my arm. It's two or three pokes-and it usually ends up that the blood has to be drawn from the back of my hand. By the time I made it to chemo, I had had so many IV's and blood draws, many of my veins had collapsed. Nurses who work at chemo facilities spend their entire day inserting IV's, and they're pros at it. Still, I was that one challenging patient who really tested their ability. At every chemo session, you are assigned one nurse who will be in charge of your treatment for that day. Annie was the designated nurse for my first treatment. I gave her a head's up about my veins, but she didn't seem worried at all. She took her first shot at getting the IV needle in, but had to remove it and try again. She checked for another viable vein, and went in a second time. "Wow, you really do have bad veins!" The second puncture *really* hurt, but apparently didn't work, either. Ditto the third. They had a rule at this facility that if the nurse was not able to get the IV successfully inserted after three tries, she had to ask another nurse to take over. That rule was implemented on me many times, including that first day.

An array of plastic bags was neatly arranged on a surgical tray next to my recliner. The treatment began with the smaller bags; they held two different types of anti-nauseates, a steroid, and a mixture of vitamins and minerals. Then came the fun part: Benadryl. When mainlined directly into your blood system, Benadryl is a potent drug. It would completely knock me out for at least an hour. I would wake up slowly, in a state of complete relaxation. It sort of felt like I was floating. I could hear voices around me, but they sounded far away. I loved that Benadryl push.

The small packets of meds were intended to minimize the horrific side effects of Taxotere and Cytoxane, my chemotherapy drugs. Those were administered in large bags that took a very long time to drain. My average chemo session lasted for about five hours.

The day after my chemo session, I returned to the treatment center to get a shot of Neulasta. Neulasta is a white cell booster that helps to avoid infection after strong chemotherapy. At this point, I was feeling pretty OK, and cautiously optimistic. Maybe I was going to be one of those rare patients who skated through chemo unfazed.

Yeah, right.

Day three after my first treatment, I awoke to some vicious side effects. My legs ached so badly, Michael had to help me get out of bed. The surface of my tongue felt like someone had used an exacto knife to make a thousand tiny cuts in it. I had to speak with a lisp, which made sound like Cindy Brady. My taste buds were messed up. No matter what I drank, it tasted like salt water. That included bottled water, tap water, carbonated water, juice, and flavored drinks. I was nauseous, dizzy, and weak. I had a raging headache. As the days passed, the symptoms gradually lessened, but I was terrified. How would I ever withstand five more sessions of chemo?

I don't know why it never occurred to me to call my oncologist. I guess I thought the adverse side effects were just a part of chemo.

I was still sick as a dog when I went in for a recheck. I climbed up onto the exam table and cocooned myself in a quilt I had brought with me. When Dr. Angstreich walked into the room, I was just a huge lump underneath the quilt. Michael was my spokesperson, rattling off answers to Dr. Angstreich's questions.

"Melissa, *never* wait to contact me when you're feeling this sick. Chemo can have some bad side effects, but there are lots of medications available that can lessen or even prevent the bad side effects. If there isn't a medication that I can call into your pharmacy, I'll ask you to come to the chemo facility and we'll figure something out. Come on, we're going to fix you up right now." The compassion he offered made me cry.

We followed Dr. A into the chemo room; a few minutes later, I was hooked up to an IV. This was my introduction to hydration therapy.

Dr. A took phenomenal care of me throughout my chemo treatments, and believe me, I was a handful. I feared that he might run out of patience with my relentless complaints and whining. I worried that I would wear on him, that he would begin rolling his eyes at the sound of my name, because I called his office on a very frequent basis. He never once failed me. He was an angel throughout my entire chemotherapy. I am still under Dr. A's care. I see him for rechecks about every six months, or if I experience any symptom that lingers for more than a few weeks. As far as I'm concerned, Dr. Angstreich not only sets the bar for any physician in any field, he far exceeds it.

Losing your hair is a cruel but usually unavoidable part of chemo. Baldness strips you of your privacy because it announces to the world that you are battling cancer. (Unless you're Sinead O'Conner.) Every time you leave your home, you have to make a choice: Wig, bandana, hat, or naked head. When I was initially diagnosed, I was distraught at the thought of losing my hair. As my journey moved forward, I came to realize that being bald wasn't that bad.

Your hair doesn't immediately fall out after your first course of chemo. It was a few weeks later when I was brushing my hair that a big clump of it came out in my hand. I brushed again harder for a minute, assuming that the rest would fall out, but it did not. I had a huge bald spot over my right ear, but the rest of my hair remained stubbornly attached to my scalp. I called my son, Eric, to ask if he still had the razor that he had used to do buzz cuts on his friends. He must have known why I was asking because his voice became soft. "Yeah, sure. You need a buzz cut, Mom?" "Yeah, I think I do, honey. A hunk of my hair just fell out, and now I have a bald spot that I can't cover up. I can't go out of the house with my hair like this." "Okay, I'll be over in a little while."

He showed up with his razor, several attachments, and some CD's.

"You know, I'm practically an expert at this. I do all of my friends' haircuts. We have a ritual, though-I have to play these songs while I work my magic." He blasted his music, danced a little, and made me laugh the entire time that my hair was falling onto the bathroom floor. What would have otherwise been a very somber time was actually a little party. I ended up with a short buzz cut, not actually bald. Eric did a great job. When he was done, he hugged me and said, "Mom, really, you look good with a buzz cut!" I have to admit it; I feared that I would resemble Uncle Fester, but I did not.

When Eric left, I decided to take this look a little bit farther. I have been changing my hair color since high school; there just happened to be one bottle of bright red hair dye in my bathroom cabinet. Of all the colors my hair had been over the years, red was Michael's favorite shade. I decided that this was the only time in my life that I could go for an Annie Lennox look. I applied the hair color and then some very heavy makeup, including false eyelashes.

Just as I was finishing up applying a coat of fire engine red lipstick, my scalp started to get really itchy. I rubbed my hands over my buzz cut, and to my horror, when I pulled them off, they were covered in tiny short red hairs. I rubbed the hair off my hands, but my head still itched, so I rubbed again. More hair fell out. I went from a buzz cut to a bald head in about thirty seconds. *Note: Your skin is extremely sensitive throughout chemo. Do not use any chemicals on any part of your body—including your head!*

I had planned on greeting Michael as Annie Lennox but that plan was now a bust. I decided to leave all my makeup on, thinking it would make the shock of seeing me bald for the first time a little less traumatic. When he walked through the front door and saw me, he stopped in his tracks, put a big smile on his face and said, "Oh wow." I could tell he was trying to gauge what *my* reaction to being bald would be. When I said, "Hey, you know how you always complain that I take way too long fussing with my hair? Guess that's not going to be an issue anymore!" He hugged me and we laughed.

Later that evening, my son Emery texted me a picture of himself. He had shaved his head in solidarity. I cried when I saw that. These were the heartwarming acts of love that carried me through my dark journey.

Later that night, I began to remove the layers of makeup from my face. When I pulled my false eyelashes off, my real eyelashes came off, too. The following day, I got that same itchy feeling in my eyebrows, and I knew what was coming. I stood over the bathroom sink and rubbed away my eyebrows. I didn't look like Uncle Fester—but I was a little concerned my appearance might frighten the neighborhood children.

It didn't stop there. Nobody had mentioned that chemo removes *all* the hair covering your body. That included legs, armpits, and hoo hoo. Sleek as a seal is what my sister Michelle, a cancer survivor, called it. Although I did look rather freakish, I sure didn't miss shaving. It took a little getting used to having a hairless hoo hoo. I tried to look on the bright side; it was a lot more hygienic.

Dr. A told me that my insurance would cover the cost of a wig. That was a very good thing, because wigs are really expensive. I wasn't even looking at real hair wigs; I was looking at a substitute that was supposed to look like real hair, and did. The wig I chose matched the color and style of what my real hair had been. It was $320.00. I wore that wig less than a dozen times. No matter how high the quality, your head can't breathe under a wig. Every time I tried to wear my wig, I would get hot flashes. I switched to hats and bandanas, which are much lighter on your head. As the weeks wore on, I began to feel more comfortable going out with a bald head. I found that people would usually just glance at me and then look away, hoping not to embarrass me, or they would catch my eye and give me a sympathetic smile. The only stares I received were from children, and that was understandable. Even the little ones who stared never said anything hurtful.

Another side effect of chemo that you don't hear a lot about is thrush. Thrush is an infection of the mucous membrane caused by the candida fungus-also known as yeast. That's right-you can get a yeast infection *in your mouth.* Dr. A had given me a head's up about thrush before my first round of chemo, but I had already seen firsthand how grotesque and diabolical this disease was.

My sister, Michelle, had a raging case of thrush during her chemo for endometrial cancer. Because she's such a trooper and always minimizes her ailments, she just tolerated a sore throat until it became unbearable. By the time she admitted that she was really sick, the thrush in her throat had been given a good long time to fester. The delay in addressing her illness caused her to be hospitalized for about a week. This is why it's imperative to contact your oncologist at the first sign of any suspicious symptoms.

Throughout her battle with endometrial cancer, Michelle was a warrior. She kept a positive attitude and refused to let cancer overtake her life. Except for her little bald head, she didn't look or act sick. That was, until the thrush outbreak.

When I walked into her hospital room, I was shocked at her appearance. She was curled up in a ball in the bed; so white she was almost translucent. Her face was covered in a sheen of sweat, but she was wrapped up in blankets because she had the chills.

I asked her to open her mouth so that I could see the source of her pain, and when she complied, I almost fainted. I was utterly unprepared for this gruesome sight. Her tongue and the roof of her mouth were covered with white, fuzzy spores. It looked exactly like the kind of mold that grows on spoiled food. This is a disease you want to avoid at all costs.

Sometime between my first and second chemo treatment, I felt a pinprick of pain in my lower gum area. When I pulled my lip down in front of the mirror, I could see a tiny white sore. It was in its infant stages, but it was thrush. I began to double down on the Biotene. Thank God, it worked.

Steroids were a part of my chemo regimen. Immediately after a chemo treatment, the steroids would give me a rush of energy. This was a frenetic energy that was hard to reign in. I became short tempered and easily annoyed at small things.

I've never been a good driver but it became increasingly difficult to control my actions when I was behind the wheel of a car. Michael dubbed this behavior, "roid rage."

One afternoon, I was driving down the street that passes in front of an elementary school. It was exactly 2:10, the end of the school day. I had a rule to avoid this street at this time. In my foggy chemo state, I had forgotten my rule.

The guard assigned to the school cross walk was about 100 years old, and had a propensity to ignore the amount of cars that would back up as she moseyed across the street with a gaggle of children. On this particular afternoon, the cars were backed up for almost an entire block. On her fourth trip, she escorted one single child across the street. I don't know what she was thinking; a large group of children were gathered together on the sidewalk, hollering and jumping up and down, impatiently waiting for their turn to cross. If the old lady took one child at a time, we all had a very long wait. I have nothing in my defense to explain what I did next, except to say, it was the steroids.

As the guard and the little girl crossed the street, I laid on the incredibly loud horn of my SUV. That tiny child flew up into the air, as if shock waves from my horn had catapulted her skyward. The crossing guard slowly turned to face my car, but remained in the middle of the street with her stop sign still held up. When I knew the little girl had safely arrived at the other side of the street, I rolled my window down and yelled out, "YOU'RE CAUSING A TRAFFIC JAM! YIELD TO THE CARS SOMETIMES, YOU DUMMY!" The guard stood frozen to the spot, her mouth gaping open and her arm still stubbornly holding up the stop sign. I made frantic motions with my arms, signaling her to get out of the way. She turned, and in her inimitable way, crossed the street at a snails pace.

Oh My God. I was out of control. I'm really surprised that none of the drivers in the cars lined up behind me didn't get out to investigate-but maybe they were afraid that I was some psycho mom. I peeled out in a huff, and hyperventilated all the way home.

The reality of what I had done didn't really sink in until I pulled into my driveway. Absolutely mortified, I began to sob and shake. What kind of a monster honks at kindergartners or 100 year-old crossing guards? When I was able to pull myself together, I walked into my house and hung up my car keys; I did not pick them up for many weeks. I decided to discontinue taking steroids; I was really past the point where they were essential. I couldn't stand the way they made me feel and look—my face was as fat as a puffer fish. I was sure I was only days away from growing facial hair and fangs.

Tom Hanks says this in the movie *Castaway*: "Coconut milk is a natural laxative; trouble is, nobody tells us about that." Like the character in that movie, I learned that lesson the hard way, too.

I knew it was crucial to stay hydrated throughout chemo, but I could not tolerate the taste of water and almost all other liquids. Everything tasted like someone had dumped a tablespoon of salt into the glass. I don't remember how I discovered coconut water, but it tasted really good. We kept our refrigerator stocked because it was my only source of hydration. I would drink as much as four quarts a day.

After my third round of chemo I began to have the worst diarrhea imaginable. I think the medical term is "urgent diarrhea." It was chronic and non–stop. My butthole would start to burn; that was my two-minute warning. Every second counted. If the dog or cats were in my way, I would yell and stomp my feet at them to move. At some point during my mad dashes, I began hollering, "Fire in the hole! Fire in the hole!" as a warning to anyone around me that I needed a clear path to the bathroom. It only took our genius border collie, Random Task, a few repetitions to catch on. Amazingly, all of our cats developed a sort of understanding of what those words meant. If one or two of them were stretched out languidly on the carpet directly in my path, they would see me running toward them, hear my declaration, and jump up onto whatever was closest to them with the swiftness and agility specific to a cat. Spartacus, our huge male cat who is as skittish as a crackhead, really hated the imposition of having to move when he was so comfortable. Sometimes he would hiss and swipe at me as I ran by him, just to let me know I was pissing him off.

I had "accidents" on a daily basis. It wasn't uncommon for me to have to change my clothes two or three times a day.

The real irony of my diarrhea was I was blamed it all on chemo. In fact, all that coconut water that I was drinking had been working like a laxative. After doing research *post* chemo, I discovered that drinking too much coconut water causes diarrhea. In essence, I would get diarrhea, and then drink lots of coconut water, believing that I was rehydrating my body. **Note: Take it easy on the coconut water.**

Last but certainly not least on my list of lesser-known side effects of chemo is a condition referred to as "chemo brain." Chemo brain is described as a decrease in mental sharpness.

Brain function problems could be caused by any one of any combination of these factors:

The cancer itself

Drugs used as part of treatment

Low blood counts

Sleep problems

Infections

Hormone changes

Hormone treatments

Nutritional deficiencies

Depression

Stress, anxiety, or emotional instability

Here are just a few symptoms of chemo brain:

Forgetting things that you usually have no trouble recalling.

Trouble concentrating.

Trouble remembering details like names, dates, and events.

Trouble multi-tasking, like answering the phone while cooking.

Taking longer to finish things.

Trouble remembering common words.

I would like to be more helpful on this subject, but I am still experiencing chemo brain. It's a miracle that I finished writing this book.

THE CANCER CARD

Moral of the chapter: Some People Will Still Be Mean

When I lost my hair from chemotherapy, I naively believed all people would be nice to me. I mean, you see a woman with a bald head, you assume she's going through chemo, right? I thought my diagnosis would come with a few benefits. I'm sorry to report that there are always going to be thoughtless, inconsiderate people who don't give a hoot that you are battling cancer.

One of the meanest people I had to deal with during chemo was a nurse who worked at the chemo facility. Go figure.

The chemo facility was state of the art. It was meticulously clean and efficient; every detail of each patient's treatment was as organized as a military operation. There were about eight nurses on staff. Following the names on their badges were many additional initials. Beyond being registered nurses, these women were highly qualified professionals who had taken many additional courses so that they were specialists in chemotherapy medicine. I think that the type of person who pursues a career in chemotherapy nursing has specific personality traits. They all seemed to be patient, compassionate, kind, and they all had a great sense of humor.

Julie, the mean nurse, was an anomaly. She caught my attention during my first chemo treatment. I noticed that she interacted with her patients differently than the other nurses. She didn't smile or make small talk. She was all business, in a Nurse Ratchett kind of way. The nurses worked on a rotation schedule, so you never knew what nurse would be assigned to take care of your treatment. Unfortunately, Julie was my designated nurse for my second treatment. I tried to be friendly at first, tried to get her to soften up, but that didn't work. She paused for a minute as she was hooking me up to the IV. In a snippy tone, she said, "Melissa, I can smell your perfume. Don't wear perfume when you come in for your treatments. Many of our patients are highly sensitive to smell. So don't wear perfume or anything scented anymore." It wasn't what she said that irked me, it was the way she said it.

"I'm not wearing perfume."

"Oh. Maybe it's your deodorant."

"I'm not wearing deodorant."

She stepped back, and in a Gestapo-like stance, scowled down at me.

"Well, you are definitely wearing something scented because I can smell something." Sniff. Sniff.

"Really? What's it smell like?"

"Hmmm, maybe vanilla?"

"Vanilla? Nope, not coming from me."

My survival instincts and I had come a long way since my cancer diagnosis. I learned to trust and use them; I honed them to perfection. They helped me be my own patient advocate. I was no longer easily intimidated, bullied, or ignored. Whether it was a doctor, Starbucks barista or store clerk, I expected to be treated in a civilized manner.

Julie knew I wasn't going to back down. She let out a loud sigh, rolled her eyes, finished hooking me up, and skulked away.

I was just about to doze off – ah, that Benadryl push -- when I suddenly remembered that I had a small bottle of antibacterial soap in my purse. I had washed my hands with it earlier. It was vanilla scented. Oh crap, Julie had been right! If she hadn't been on her high horse, I would have apologized. But I didn't. However, I never used that soap again.

My second infraction, according to Julie, was bringing an inappropriate food item to my chemo station. I'm not kidding. Michael had walked to a deli that was a few blocks from the chemo facility, and I asked him to bring me back a turkey sandwich. The sandwich consisted of roasted turkey, cheddar cheese, a tomato slice, and lettuce. It was on a small French baguette roll. It did not contain mustard, onion, or any kind of stinky cheese. Julie, who wasn't even my designated nurse that day, happened to walk past my chair and saw the lunch bag sitting on the metal tray next to me. She stopped directly in front of me and asked what was in the bag.

I momentarily considered asking her if she was the fucking lunch bag police. I had an IV of toxic medications dripping into my bloodstream. I was tired, bald, sweaty, and hungry, and I didn't feel like being harassed.

"It's a sandwich."

"What kind of a sandwich?"

"Julie, why do you need to know what kind of a sandwich I have?" Honestly, I don't know why I didn't just answer her question. I was having a bad day. Or maybe it was because she was standing so close in front of me that our knees were practically touching. I felt like she was invading my personal space, and I wanted to push back. She bent forward slightly.

" I'm asking you what kind of a sandwich that is because if it has anything in it that has a strong odor, it could make the patients around you nauseous. You have to be considerate of others."

What made her think I was an inconsiderate nitwit? Of course I knew better than to bring some stinky food item into the facility!

"OK. I get it. It's not tuna fish, it's not egg salad, and it doesn't have any kind of stinky cheese on it." I was acting like a petulant child. I needed my Benadryl push. Badly.

She remained stubbornly planted in front of me, and I wanted to dig into that sandwich, so I let her win.

"It's a turkey sandwich. It has lettuce, tomato, alfalfa sprouts, and cheddar cheese. There's nothing stinky on that sandwich. If you want to inspect it, I'm going to have to insist that you put on a fresh pair of gloves. You must be a hotbed of *germs*." (I shuddered a little, to convey my horror at what she must be carrying.)

"Well, seriously, Melissa! I would never ask to inspect your sandwich! I'm just doing my job; I'm trying to make this place as comfortable as possible for all our patients. This is a petrifying time for the people in this room, you know."

"Julie, do you not see this IV?" (I dramatically swung my arm out so that she could see the ugly rainbow of bruises and needle tracks.) "*I am one of those petrified people!*" I should have let it go, but her last remark infuriated me.

She shrugged and began to walk away, but I was on a roll here. I raised my voice and called after her:

"Hey Julie, wait. I have a question."

Turns, rolls her eyes, hunches her shoulders forward.

"What?"

"I noticed that the nurses have food catered in at lunchtime every

Friday."

"That's right, we do. Friday is a half day; we have lunch catered in from different restaurants and we all eat together."

"Yeah, I know. You know how I know? Because every Friday afternoon, the smell of whatever you guys ordered for lunch comes wafting out here. Last week it was Mexican, right?"

That deer in the headlight expression immediately crossed Julie's face. She knew exactly where I was going with this.

"Ummmmm…I don't really remem…actually, yeah, I think it was Mexican."

"Julie, you've got a lot of nerve. You sniff around this place like a bomb detecting K9. But every Friday, the staff orders stinky food with no regard to its potent smell---a smell that all the patients hooked up to IV's have to endure. Maybe you ladies should be a little more considerate about the type of food you have catered in. And for God's sake, close the door to the lunch room!" Nailed! Take that! She turned around and stomped off.

Evidently, someone overheard our little spat. The following Friday, when the stinky Chinese food that the nurses ordered arrived, they made sure the door to their lounge area was kept tightly closed.

My third and fourth infractions were exceeding the limit of visitors per treatment, and laughing during a treatment. I'm not making this stuff up.

My sister, Michelle, had dropped by during one of my treatments. We were talking back and forth, not loudly, and every now and then, we would laugh. Not guffaw, not roar. We would softly laugh. About half an hour passed, and Julie, again not my designated nurse of the day, headed our direction with a sour look on her face. I could see it coming.

"Melissa, you can only have one visitor during your treatment. This room is too small to accommodate any more than that."

Well, that was for sure. This place didn't even offer a chair for the friend or family member who accompanied the chemo patient. The only seating available was the occasional unused wheeled stool that the technicians sat on. There were many times when Michael had to remain standing next to my chemo station for four or five hours.

"I only have one visitor."

"No. You have that person there"- pointing to Michelle-"and your husband. That's two."

"My husband? My husband is downstairs."

"Well yes, but that's two visitors."

"I don't think it counts as a "visitor" if my husband is downstairs. His body isn't taking any space up here, right?"

Michelle stood up and walked over to a window, pretending to be gazing outside. I could see her shoulders shaking, and I worried for a moment that she was crying. Then I heard the snort, and I knew she was laughing her ass off.

Julie walked over to Michelle, got right in her face, and chastised her. "Excuse me- You are being very inconsiderate! I hope I don't have to ask you to leave!"

We had been having a quiet conversation, interspersed with soft laughter. I could not understand how that sound would be at all objectionable to any other patients in the room. In fact, I should imagine it would be uplifting.

Michelle left shortly after Julie's tongue lashing. As she walked toward the exit, she put an exaggerated bounce in her step, and it almost looked like she was skipping. She looked over at Julie with an ear-to-ear grin. I laughed so hard I peed my pants.

When Michael returned from downstairs, he asked why Michelle was leaving so soon. Julie was within earshot, and I wanted her to hear me. "Well, honey, I guess it's against the rules to laugh around here." My next round of chemo, Michelle snuck in and hid from Julie. We tried very hard not to laugh.

It always made a treatment seem faster and easier if the people who were seated next to you were friendly. During one of my hydration treatments, I was seated next to a very sweet elderly woman. We struck up a conversation, and as we were chatting, Julie walked by. My new lady friend immediately recoiled, the way a turtle retreats into its shell when sensing danger. When Julie was out of earshot, the woman leaned toward me and whispered, "Oh, I don't like that one at all! She's so mean!"

"I know! She's been mean to me, too!"

"She made me cry!"

"She made you *cry*? What did she do?"

"Well, I kept getting my IV line knotted up, and she got upset because she kept having to reset my machine. She came over and yelled at me and threatened to tie my arm down to the chair if I made the buzzer go off again!"

I wasn't surprised in the least that Julie had been mean to this sweet little lady, but I was shocked that she would actually threaten a patient.

"I think threatening a patient might be grounds for termination! Did you report this to someone?"

"No! I was afraid that if I got her in trouble, she would be even meaner to me!"

I completely understood her paradox. You don't want to be at the mercy of a meanie, but you also don't want the person who is in charge of your treatment to be angry with you. Consider the power this person has over you. This nurse is responsible for hooking you up to your IV-they draw your blood; they stick a needle deep into your veins. The rule at this facility was each nurse had three tries to get that IV needle in place. If they were unable to do so, they were supposed to call another nurse to take over. It was up to the nurse to give a shout out if she had used up her three tries. What if she decided not to do that? What if she jabbed you four times, or five? The hooking up to the IV is the most painful part of the chemo treatment-you definitely want the person who is holding the needle to like you.

I urged this lady to report this incident to her physician, or at least request that Julie not be assigned as her nurse for any more treatments. I don't know if she followed through with my advice. I had my own final blow out with Julie the following week.

I was very near the end of my treatments. Chemo had taken its toll. I felt beat up and exhausted beyond description. Every joint and bone in my body ached, my butthole was sore, and my taste buds were AWOL, causing everything to taste like cardboard. I was under the care of an ophthalmologist because the Taxotere was wreaking havoc on my eyes. I had an ongoing bladder irritation. I was at my lowest point, physically and emotionally. I even remember asking Dr. A if it was absolutely necessary for me to have my fourth treatment. Unfortunately, he insisted that it was.

I knew I was on the verge of a major meltdown. I sat in my chemo station waiting to be hooked up for my hydration therapy. I tensed up when it became apparent that Julie would be my designated nurse for that session. Not only had she been assigned to me; I could tell she was on the warpath.

The steel tray that should have held all the necessary meds for my session was not complete. When Julie realized this, she stomped back to the lab to procure the missing items. She returned shortly, but then knocked something off the tray and had to throw it away because it was no longer sterile. That necessitated a second trip back to the lab. By the time she began the complicated process of assembling my IV meds, she was gritting her teeth. Just as she was finishing up, she stopped fiddling with all the lines and looked down at me.

"Why are you here today?"

I was so taken aback by that ignorant question I repeated it back to her.

"Why am I here today?"

"Yes. Why are you here today?"

I was there for hydration therapy. The small plastic packets that she was hanging on my IV pole were a clear indicator as to why I was there.

"I'm here for hydration."

"Why are you here for hydration?"

"Um, I'm here for hydration because I don't feel good." She raised her voice by several decibels, drawing the attention of the patients around me.

"NO! I know you don't feel good! HOW don't you feel good?"

All of my spunk and sassy sat mute on the back of my tongue. Chemo brain took over. I couldn't access the right words, couldn't connect to the adjectives that would adequately describe my symptoms. I just kept drawing a blank. I began repeating myself like an annoying parrot:

"I...I just don't feel good... I don't... feel good."

"I know you don't feel good! WHAT ARE YOUR SYMPTOMS?"

There were times during my battles with cancer when I temporarily imploded. I would briefly give in to a deep, black hopelessness or a terror so profound it took my breath away. On one of these occasions, I collapsed on our kitchen floor and began sobbing so hard that the sounds coming out of me didn't sound human. Our Border collie, Random Task, was in the adjoining room. These otherworldly sounds startled him. He walked into the kitchen with his head hung low and his ears pinned back, and cautiously made his way over to me. He laid down next to me and put his head on my lap. I could feel his whole body trembling, the way it did when the firecrackers began to boom on the fourth of July. My outburst was freaking him out. I hugged him close and spoke to him in a soothing voice until both of our terrors were gone.

One early evening in late May, I stood on our back yard deck, screaming a torrent of my grievances out to God at the top of my lungs. I hadn't realized that my neighbor was starting up his BBQ in his adjacent backyard. I caught the movement of his body out of the corner of my eye; he left his yard and very quietly closed the sliding door behind him.

I remember a phone call from a very dear friend. She quite innocently and sincerely asked me how I was holding up. I answered that I wished I would just die and get it over with.

I was feeling broken and forlorn on this particular day. I didn't have the fortitude to banter with Julie. Instead, I hung my head and began to cry softly. Between sobs, I would offer up a symptom.

"I...hurt everywhere." Sniffle.

"I'm too tired to move." Quick intake of shaky breath.

"I can't go anywhere fun!" A stifled sob.

"It feels like I have sand in my eyes all the time. I can't read, I can't paint, I can't write!" With each symptom that I named, I began to cry harder.

"My teeth hurt."

"One of my chemo meds is irritating my bladder. I feel like I constantly have a burning urinary tract infection!"

For the piece de resistance: "I have out of control diarrhea! I poop my pants all the time! My butthole is so raw it hurts to sit down!" With this last symptom, I began to howl like a wounded wolf.

The sound of my wails echoed throughout the room. All the nurses left their posts to come over to comfort me. They bent down and put their arms around me so that I was the center of a big group hug. When I regained my composure, my circle of support went back to their stations. Only Julie remained.

"Melissa, how often do you come in for hydration therapy?"

"It varies. It depends upon how I'm feeling. Doctor Angstreich told me that I could come in as often as I wanted to, every day if it was making me feel better. He said that IV hydrating is really good for me. I always feel so much better after hydration."

"Hmmm… really?" She was attaching the final plastic pouch to my IV.

"I'm just asking because, you know, all you're getting during these treatments is water. It's just water with a little salt in it. There's really no proven medical benefit in getting an IV drip of water. Just drink a lot of water at home-you'll get the same results."

Michael had made a trip to the restroom and missed all the action. But he could tell something nasty had transpired while he was gone because I looked like a hot mess. Since Julie was my nurse, he figured she was the culprit. Before he could ask any questions, I said, "Hey honey, Julie here was just telling me that drinking water orally gives you the exact same results as having IV hydration."

Michael frowned and looked at Julie.

"That's not true."

"No, it is true! Melissa's IV bag is just water with a little salt in it. If she just drinks a lot of water, she would get the same results at home."

Michael rolled his eyes.

"Julie, that is *not true*."

"She might *think* she feels better after her hydration therapy, but you know, that's really in her head. Drinking a lot of water orally would give her the exact same results as being hooked up to an IV of water."

Was she implying I was a head case?

Michael's face flushed a bright red. I was expecting him to raise his voice, but instead, he hissed at Julie. Hissed, like a snake. I can't remember exactly what he said, but it was something along these lines:

"Julie, I'm sick and tired of your bad attitude. I'm sick and tired of watching you be rude to your patients. You never smile. You never have anything nice to say. I appreciate that you are well credentialed, but no matter how many initials you have on your badge, your personality should exempt you from working in a chemotherapy facility."

Julie stood there with her mouth gaping open. I don't think anyone had ever given her a dressing down like that.

"And you, of all people, should know that when a person drinks water, it has to go through their digestive track before it gets absorbed into their bloodstream. An IV of water is mainlined *directly* into your bloodstream. It's got a completely different effect. This is really basic science, Julie. You should know this stuff."

Michael's face wasn't red anymore, but Julie's was. She was furious, but smart enough to know if she started an argument with a scientist who majored in organic chemistry, she would lose.

That afternoon, we spoke to Dr. Angstreich and I never had to deal with Julie again.

For any chemo nurses who are reading this, I applaud your sincere desire to help people through the worst times of their lives. A good chemo nurse is nothing short of an angel, and deserves the utmost in respect and gratitude. I realize that Julie was an anomaly, but you have to be prepared for people like her. If you're walking around with a bald head, battling some form of cancer, you may assume that everyone you encounter will be compassionate and caring. Unfortunately, you're still going to come across thoughtless, rude, inconsiderate, people who don't give a hoot about your disease. Losers.

Part Two

King Me

THE BEST MEDICINE

Moral of the Chapter: Find Something That Inspires You

Reactions to chemotherapy are as diverse as the patients who undergo this treatment. Some patients spend the entire course of their therapy in bed, weak, nauseous, feverish and miserable. Other patients breeze through chemo. I've heard many stories of women who still continued to do their daily three-mile run or workout routine at the gym. A friend of mine who underwent eight sessions of an extremely aggressive chemo regimen was able to keep up with her tennis team.

I was in the waiting room of my plastic surgeon's office one afternoon, and sitting next to me was a strikingly beautiful woman with a bald head. I loved that she had made no effort to cover her baldness. This was just prior to my surgery, so I had a lot of questions about what to expect in the months to come. When I got up the nerve to engage this woman in a conversation, I asked her what chemo had been like for her. She said it was extremely variable and unpredictable. The day after her second treatment, she hosted a Thanksgiving dinner for sixty guests with no problems. On her bad days, she said taking her pain medication and soaking in a hot tub were the only things that relieved her of the excruciating head to toe aches. One afternoon, when she had been too weak to get up off her sofa, her eight-year old son remarked that when she was having a bad day, she was "like a puddle." For some reason, I remembered that comment, and it turned out to be a perfect description of the kind of fatigue that is common to chemotherapy.

In April 2012, when my chemotherapy began, I expected to be tired and nauseated, as that seemed to be the most common complaints from survivors. However, I thought I would be able to read and write and paint throughout my treatments. I had neither heard nor read of anyone experiencing vision problems. Unfortunately, after my first round of chemo, adverse side effects from the Taxotere began to wreak havoc on my eyes. I either had tears running down my face, and completely blurred vision, or my eyes were so dry and completely devoid of any moisture that when I blinked, I could feel my eyelids scratching my eyeballs. When I reported these symptoms to Dr. A., he knew exactly what the source of the problem was. My mucosal system was under attack. That same word that my former OB/GYN had used was making a comeback. Apparently, we have mucous membranes throughout our body, including our eyes.

Writing, painting, sewing, crafting, and reading were out of the question. For the first few weeks, my life consisted of watching DVD's. I found that comedy made me feel a little better; I lost count of how many times I watched *Swingers, Office Space, Happy Gilmore,* and *First in Show.*

When my energy level began to return, I wandered around the house, trying to figure out what to do with myself.

I needed something to inspire me. Inspiration brings enthusiasm, encouragement, and motivation. It provides a person with a reason to get up, get dressed, and get out. Through a bizarre twist of events, my inspiration came from The Los Angeles Kings.

My sons, Eric and Emery, stopped by one evening in late April to check up on me. I bemoaned the fact that I had watched all my comedy DVD's, my favorites over and over again.

Eric suggested that I start following the Stanley Cup playoffs. This year, the Los Angeles Kings were contenders for the Cup.

In 1990, when Eric was in high school, he made friends with a new student who had moved to Southern California from Saskatchewan, Canada. Landon Wilson ended up in our tiny berg of El Segundo because his father, Rick, had been hired to be the assistant coach for the Los Angeles Kings.

Hockey was a much less popular sport in Los Angeles back then. The Anaheim Ducks did not exist, nor did the San Jose Sharks. In 1988, when Wayne Gretzky was added to the roster of The Los Angeles Kings, the popularity of the sport began to climb here. People who knew nothing about hockey knew the name Wayne Gretzky. His earned moniker, *The Great One*, said it all.

The Wilson family had deep roots in ice hockey. Rick had played in the NHL for many years, his wife was a power skating coach, and Landon was in ice skates at the age of three. Like his father, his dream was to play in the NHL.

I liked Landon very much. He was a hulking young man with a shy nature and a heart of gold. His manners were very refreshing. He answered my questions with a "Yes, Ma'am" or "No, Ma'am" and always offered to help clean up after dinner. (Eric discouraged this. "Hey dude, she's gonna expect *me* to do that now!") I heartily encouraged this friendship, hoping that Landon's wonderful qualities would rub off on my own sons.

I knew Eric was spending a lot of time in skating rinks with Landon, but I always thought he was just a spectator. Up until this time, I don't think Eric had ever ice-skated. Both my sons are fearless risk takers with little regard to bodily harm; I shouldn't have been surprised when Eric admitted he was playing hockey alongside Landon. The minute he fessed up, I began to beg him to let me come watch him play. He held me off for as long as he could, but eventually gave in to my incessant pleas.

When I finally got permission to go to a game, it came with a long list of unacceptable behaviors. This included, but was not limited to; yelling out his name, cheering for him, waving to him, or going anywhere near the ice to say hello to him. Pretty much, he just wanted me to act like we didn't know each other. A typical request.

At that time, the only thing that I understood about hockey was that the objective of the game was to hit the little black thing into the net. About two minutes into my first game, I learned that hockey is a very complex sport. It's not like baseball, a fairly straightforward game where you watch the pitcher, the batter, and any players on base. It's not like basketball or golf, where you just have to keep your eyes on the ball. Everything about hockey moves at lightening speed. That little black thing, the puck, is often difficult to track because it's so small, is usually surrounded by players, and in constant motion. The players are continually changing up, leaping over the bench to charge the ice, playing for about two minutes, and then scooting back to the bench. The referees blow their whistles non stop, and then make a myriad of different signals with their arms. I seriously needed a copy of Hockey For Dummies.

That was OK, though, because I was really only there to watch Eric play this new sport. When his team skated out onto the ice, I could hardly believe my eyes. I know I sound like a bragging mom here, but this is true: My son, who had only been playing hockey for a few months, was just as graceful and swift as all the other players. It was amazing to watch him zoom up and down the rink, and glide elegantly along the sideboards. I held my breath for a second when he began to skate backwards at full speed. Nothing about his skating screamed *rookie*.

Sitting in the first row of bleachers was a mistake; I was close enough to hear the breath being knocked out of the players and the groans of pain when they were slammed into the sideboards. This sport was downright brutal. Hockey sticks were not just for hitting the puck, they doubled as weapons. They were used to trip, hook, and smack an opponent.

Eric had explained "chirping" to me. Chirping is when two opponents talk smack to each other, trying to get a rise out of one another. It's easy to read the lips of the guys on the ice; I wasn't surprised or shocked at the exchange of colorful language. My husband has the foulest mouth of anyone I know.

The other aspect of hockey Eric had warned me about was a phenomena known as "dropping the gloves." Dropping the gloves closely resembles a bar brawl. Two players suddenly stop in their tracks and face each other. They drop their gloves, and begin swinging furiously at each other. A referee stands a few feet away from the fracas, nonchalantly monitoring the fight until it has to be broken up. This was the only sport that I knew of where fighting was allowed.

Toward the end of the second period, seemingly out of nowhere, two players stopped in the middle of the ice and began circling one another. There was a little pushing and shoving, and then I saw the gloves flying. The players began to duke it out. The helmets went flying. There were some vicious punches going back and forth; these guys weren't fooling around. The players on both teams were smacking their hockey sticks against the ice and cheering their teammate on. The ref just stood there, cool as a cucumber, allowing the hitting to go on and on. When he finally stepped in, the combatants took off in separate directions. One of them headed back to his teammates, the other skated off the ice while using his jersey to staunch the flow of blood that was pouring from his nose. I can't stand the sight of blood. My stomach flipped when that kid skated past me.

I could never make it as a hockey mom. I was never the kind of parent who could sit quietly during any sport when either of my sons was unfairly hit or at the receiving end of a bad call. I was the mom screaming from the bleachers if I felt any injustice had been perpetrated on my boys. I was the mom who would walk down to the dugout to say something inspirational to my boy if he dropped an easy fly ball and was now the scourge of the team. I never understood the kind of mom who would ridicule her child from the stands. I felt that if a child was already struggling, publicly humiliating them was like rubbing salt in their wounds.

Later that season, I was at one of Eric's games when a teammate was violently shoved into the sideboard. I could see him grimacing in pain as he held his arm against his body and skated over to the woman sitting next to me. "Hey Mom! I think I broke my arm!" If that had been Eric, I would have had him in my car and on the way to the closest E.R. in a heartbeat. This woman didn't even flinch; she just yelled back, "Get back on that ice!" I wanted to smack her silly. I definitely didn't have what it takes to be a hockey mom.

This was exactly the reason that Eric had waited so long to invite me to a game. He knew I was as protective as a mama bear. After witnessing my first hockey fight, I had to watch the remainder of the game through fingers laced over my eyes. By the end of the first period, I was as drained as the players on the ice.

When Eric graduated from high school, he chose to attend college in North Dakota. His choice of college was based strictly on the ability to play hockey. It soon became apparent that he was spending more time in the rink than he was in any classroom. His grades were mediocre. At the end of his second year, he realized that as much as he loved playing hockey, he had started playing the game at far too old an age. Professional hockey players begin their careers as very young children, as young as three years old. Also, he was sick of those bitter grey North Dakota winters that seemed to last forever.

I was ecstatic when he returned home.

Still, hockey was Eric's true passion. He continued to play through a variety of different avenues as often as he could. I really wanted to have a better understanding of this sport he loved so much. One afternoon, he patiently walked me through the basics of the game. He began by drawing a diagram of a hockey rink on a piece of paper and then placing some tiny plastic army men on top of that. He explained what the lines on the ice meant, what the positions of the players were called, and the job of each player. He talked about the strategy behind some of the plays. He explained what the hand signals from the referees meant. Over the years, he's taught me so much. The more I learn, the more I realize there is still so much to learn.

Our entire family joined Eric in becoming die-hard LA Kings fans. When the Kings were making a run for the Stanley cup in 1993, we all gathered around the TV set to cheer them on.

Landon Wilson, who had opened up the world of ice hockey to my family, made it to the NHL. We were all so proud of him.

Somehow, over the years, I lost touch with hockey. It was nineteen years later when Eric suggested that I follow the Stanley Cup playoffs. The Los Angeles Kings were four games into the quarterfinals, and were ahead three to one. In their 45-year history the Kings had yet to win the most coveted trophy in the NHL. This definitely intrigued me. It would be exhilarating to see our team victoriously hoist that coveted silver cup over their heads. I've always been a sucker for the underdog.

On April 22, 2012, I tuned in to watch the Kings versus The Vancouver Canucks. It was the fifth game of the Western Conference Quarterfinals. I was immediately immersed in the action. Any thoughts about cancer, chemotherapy, radiation, or dying, disappeared; my energy and focus were strictly on the game. At the end of the third period, the score was tied 1-1. What could be more exciting than going into overtime during a championship game?

Slightly over four minutes into overtime, with a quick flick of his wrists, Jarrett Stoll slammed the puck into the net. BOOM! The LA Kings secured a spot in the Stanley Cup Semi-Finals.

I ran out to my front yard and started running around in circles, whooping "GO KINGS GO! GO KINGS GO! GO KINGS GO!" My neighbors may have thought my bizarre behavior was some side effect of chemo. Michael was yelling at me to come back inside, but I ignored his pleas. I knew I looked like a lunatic, but I just couldn't contain my euphoria.

Watching the game had provided a perfect reprieve from my ever-present anxiety and fear. You can't be wrapped up in a hot game of hockey and think about your personal problems, no matter how grim they may be.

The Los Angeles Kings became my inspiration.

INTREPID SPIRIT

Moral of the chapter: What Lies Behind You And What Lies Ahead Of You Is Nothing Compared To What Lies Within You

Mahatma Gandhi

A cancer diagnosis will change you in a myriad of ways. Life's daily annoyances, things that used to drive you crazy, become completely inconsequential. You quit arguing your point until you win the debate, because it just seems like a waste of energy. You let people cut you off while driving without needing to honk your horn and flip them off. If you notice someone behind you in a checkout line with one or two items, and your cart is full, you offer to let them take cuts. You are never in that big of a hurry.

I changed in all those ways, and so many more. I actually wrote up a "bucket list." If presented the opportunity to do something on that list, I took it. The scope of my life became much more vast.

Near the top of my bucket list was going to a LA Kings game. I knew tickets would be pricey, but I had no idea to what degree hockey had caught on in Los Angeles. The fan base had blossomed, and it was playoff time-the most expensive time of the season. Ticket availability was limited to either nosebleed seats or seats that were fetching as much as $2000 each. Michael would've done anything to bring me some happiness during that horrible time; I was the one who kept hesitating to buy tickets.

I remembered that my niece my niece, Tiffany, had married into a family of passionate LA Lakers fans. Don Esmond, Tiffany's father-in-law, was a high-powered executive at Toyota Motors. One of the perks of his position was access to executive suites at the Staples Center. For many years, Tiffany and her family made almost weekly treks to the Lakers games, enjoying all the VIP treatment that came along with being in a suite.

I had no idea if Don would be able to procure tickets to a Kings game, but I was willing to swallow my pride and ask. I emailed Tiffany to ask if Don could get tickets to any of the Kings playoff games. I told her to tell him that they were for her aunt who was battling breast cancer. I told her to mention that I was in chemo. I told her to lay it on really thick.

Tiffany was more than happy to oblige but warned me that playoff game tickets were much harder to come by. She didn't want me to get my hopes up. I went back to the Internet and continued to look for tickets.

She called me a few hours later. I don't know how in the world they pulled this off, but Don and his wife, Cheryl, offered to take us to the next Kings game. Not only were we going to the game, we were going to be sitting in ice seats. Ice seats are the first row in the arena, directly behind the Plexiglas that separates the rink from the spectators. These tickets are reserved exclusively for VIPs.

I couldn't wait for Michael to get home. As soon as he walked through the front door, I screamed out that we were going to the game AND that we would be sitting in ice seats. "Ice seats? Does that mean we'll be sitting on the ice?"

"Well, no honey, I don't think the seats are actually on the ice—but they are in the first row!" His expression was one of utter joy, until he thought about it for a minute. "Wait. What day is this game?" "Thursday." "Did you forget that you have chemo on Monday?" In fact, I had completely forgotten that I had chemo on Monday. After my first session, I had not been able to get out of bed for a week. I had no way of knowing how I would be feeling after the second treatment, but there was no way on this earth that I was going to miss the opportunity to go to a Kings playoff game, and sit in ice seats like a rock star.

"Sweetie, you may have to roll me to our seats in a wheelchair, but we're going to that game."

"What if your white blood cell count is too low? Right now you have almost no immune system. I'm not sure if it's a good idea to expose yourself to 18,000 fans. Can you imagine what must float through the air in that arena?"

"There are ways that I can protect myself from all the germs! I can wear gloves. I can use antibacterial soap. I won't touch any surfaces. I'll only breathe out." I began to panic. Michael, my ever-vigilant guardian angel, my patient advocate who took notes and did research and kept calm when I wasn't able to, was keeping his feet planted firmly in common sense while I was focusing only on the awesomeness of going to the game.

"Okay. You have chemo on Monday. We'll go back Tuesday for your Neulasta injection, take Wednesday off, and go back on Thursday for hydration therapy. If your treatment goes well, and you are strong enough, *and* if Dr. Angstreich says it's OK, we'll go." I nodded enthusiastically, but in my head I was thinking, come hell or high water, I am going to that game.

On Monday, April 30, 2012, I had my second chemotherapy treatment. Based on how my body reacted to the first series of chemotherapy drugs, Dr. Angstreich made a few adjustments. I was praying the second round would not be as hard as the first.

We followed Michael's game plan. On Tuesday, I went back for my

Neulasta injection. I also received hydration therapy. I rested on Wednesday, and we went back on Thursday morning for another IV of hydrating medications. I think I asked Dr. Angstreich to add a little extra steroid medication, because this was the medication used to build up strength and resistance in chemo patients. We had already discussed the hockey game with Dr. Angstreich. Every time I went to the chemo facility, my blood was drawn and extensive lab tests were run. That day, my white cell count was very low, but Dr. Angstreich understood how desperately I wanted to go to that game. He gave me the go-ahead, reminding me to wear gloves and try to avoid standing in a large crowd of people. I promised him I would only breathe out.

On May 3, 2012, the Los Angeles Kings hosted The St. Louis Blues for the third game of the semi-final playoffs. Michael and I pulled into the VIP parking lot at the Staples Center, which was the closest parking structure to the Staples Center. For a healthy person, the walk is actually quite brief. I was not a healthy person. We weren't even out of the parking structure, and my legs were starting to burn. Michael, who typically walks as if there is a fire behind him, had adopted a more leisurely pace since my diagnosis. He held my arm as we walked at a snails pace towards The Staples Center.

Fortunately, there was a small brick retaining wall surrounding the entrance. I had to sit down for a few minutes because it felt as if there were 20 pound sandbags tied around both my ankles. I rested until I felt I had the strength to continue on. The walk to our seats seemed to go on and on, corridor after corridor; it finally ended when we entered a private elevator that descended to the ice rink level. Once we exited the elevator, it was easy to find the way to our seats. There was a short tunnel that had a thick black curtain at the end of it. I didn't know it at the time, but this tunnel is the same route that the team uses when exiting their locker room and heading onto the ice. I wish I had known back then that I was walking on such hallowed ground. I would have taken a picture.

The black curtain had two security guards flanking each side. No fans were allowed past this point without proof of being a VIP. I proudly handed our tickets over. The guard studied them quite seriously for a moment. He reminded me of Mr. T, huge, greatly muscled, bald, with a slight scowl on his face. Did he know we were poseurs, just regular folk pretending to be rock stars? Did he think the tickets were fake, or worse, stolen? As the seconds ticked on, I began to sweat. I was a mere few feet away from realizing a dream; if this man blocked my path, I would have to cause the biggest scene in the history of the Staples Center. When he finally handed our tickets back to me, his expression changed. A huge smile covered his face. He offered me his arm. "Welcome to the Staples Center! Madame? May I show you to your seat?" With those words he reached over and in one highly dramatic movement, snapped that heavy black curtain open.

I took his arm and we were led to our seats. If I weren't so weak, I would've skipped.

The ice seat row consists of fold out chairs, a split of four and four. The chairs are elevated by two steps, and surrounded on all sides by a railing that prevents interlopers from gaining access. The distance between the fold out chairs and the Plexiglas is about two feet. Not only were these ice seats, these were ice seats in section 103, which is a mere one section away from the LA Kings bench. Simply put, we were pretty much in the best seats in the house.

Don and Cheryl had already arrived. Don sat on the aisle seat, Cheryl next to him. I hugged them both before I sat down. We had only met them a few times. Don had a military background; he generally maintains a very serious expression on his face and has the best posture I had ever seen. Cheryl had been raised on a farm in the Midwest; you could still sense a little bit of the farm girl in her. She's very genuine and down to earth. Their family was devoutly religious. These were the type of Christians that honored and celebrated God in their daily lives. I did not find out until the third period the trouble to which they had gone to fulfill my wish of going to a hockey game.

Shortly after the game began, Cheryl began asking me some pretty basic questions. Why did two players have an "A" on their jersey? What did "icing," mean? What did the gestures from the referee mean? She seemed to know very little about the game, so I asked her how many times she and Don had been to a Kings game. "Oh, never." They weren't even hockey fans! The reason they were at the game was because guests were not allowed access to the VIP sections unless their hosts were also in attendance. As the game progressed, I noticed that Cheryl was rubbing her knee a lot. I asked her about that and she told me that she had undergone knee surgery three days prior to the game; the icy cold air surrounding us was making her knee ache. I felt terrible! Not only had she dragged herself to a sports event that she wasn't even interested in, but she was recovering from knee surgery! Also, she and Don had driven from Newport Beach to downtown Los Angeles during the height of rush-hour traffic. It had taken them more than two hours to drive one way. How can you not believe in angels when people like this appear in your life? Don and Cheryl Esmond, thank you for one of the best nights of my life.

We arrived early enough so that we would be able to watch the Kings during their pregame practice session. Thirty minutes before the game began, I could hear the thunder of the players stampeding down the tunnel that was about three feet to my left. They were so close I could have reached out and touched them as they passed.

Drew Doughty, whose stats made him one of the leading defenseman that season, was skating directly in front of me. It was riveting to watch how he could move around on the ice. I think because he spent so much time on the ice, his body didn't really feel a difference between being on ice or being on solid ground. His skates were just an extension of his body.

In the section adjacent to ours, a small herd of children had smooshed their bodies against the plexiglass in an attempt to get as close as possible to their idols. Drew would glide along the sideboard and use the blades of his skates to shoot a spray of ice up at the children. This would elicit screams of joy.

I watched as he would throw his head back and laugh with a childlike abandon; he sang and danced along to the piped in music, he snapped his bubble gum and twirled his hockey stick like a Keystone cop. He would look up at the adult fans lined six deep around the ice and flash a great big smile. His front tooth was missing, but I think he wore that like a badge of honor. Having your teeth knocked out came with the territory. That Drew obviously loved this game and openly appreciated his fans gave him a kind of mojo. All these thoughts were running through my mind when I suddenly realized he was looking over at me. Had I been staring at him? I averted my eyes. I didn't want him to be creeped out by an old lady staring holes through him.

I turned my attention to the goalie, Jonathon Quick, who was crouching in the crease of the net. Goalie gear weighs between forty and fifty pounds, and covers that player from head to toe. With all that protective padding "Quickie" resembled the Michelin Man. Only a small slice of his upper face was uncovered, exposing his dark, piercing eyes. They followed the path of every puck that shot down the ice at him like a speeding bullet. While the other players on the ice appeared relaxed, Quickie was already in game mode. I later learned that some hockey players could shoot a puck upwards of one hundred hours per hour. The average amount of weight a goalie loses per game is ten pounds. I found everything about that position fascinating.

Back then I would not have known the difference between a good goalie, a great goalie, and the best goalie in the NHL. But even a rookie fan like me could see that Jonathon Quick had the reflexes and agility of a cat. Sports commentators referred to his talent as "exceptional athleticism" and "superior lateral moves." Those are descriptions from the professionals. What I would have said is that Quickie moved like Gumby. I had never seen a body do what he was able to do; contort, jump, slide, and shift around the goalie crease with precision and at lightening speed. I would watch a puck scream down the ice toward him, and literally, in the blink of an eye, he would be standing up with the puck tucked snugly into his glove. I could barely believe my eyes when several of his teammates started firing pucks at him simultaneously, and he was still able to block those shots. When Michael and I made it to the top of the season ticket member waiting list, we chose seats that were as close to Quickie as we could get. We both felt it was more exciting to observe the genius of Jonathon Quick than to watch our team score a goal.

When the practice period was over, the team tromped back down the tunnel leading to their locker room. The arena lights were brought down. Psychedelic purple and lime green laser lights began to flash through the darkened air. "The Black Parade" by My Chemical Romance was softly playing; up on the Jumbotron, a video opened with the words, " *A Childhood Dream*." The first image on the immense screen was a stick drawing of a hockey game in progress. Childhood pictures of Dustin Brown and Drew Doughty followed. The next words were, "*A lifetime of waiting.*" Childhood pictures of Jonathon Quick flickered across the screen, and the crowd went wild. In rapid succession, snippets of different players, at varying ages, flashed before our eyes. The words, "*An Opportunity*" appeared, with more pictures of players. The crowd went wild for the second time when clips of the Stanley Cup came into view. The video ended with the phrase "*It's Our Time*"; I had tears streaming down my face before the game even began.

When the teams returned to the ice, the fans rose to their feet, clapping and stomping and screaming. I had never seen nor heard such fevered enthusiasm. I closed my eyes and let the feeling in that arena wash over me. I wanted to soak up as much of that positive energy as I could.

We were only seconds into the game when I realized that without the color commentating by Jim Fox, the play-by-play announcing by Bob Miller, and a cameraman to track the puck, I was lost. My eyes and brain couldn't process what was unfolding in real time.

Michael and I sometimes feel a pang of regret when we reflect back on our first game and those awesome ice seats. We had such a limited understanding of hockey and the stats of the players on our team. We've learned so much over the years; if we were able to sit in those ice seats again, it would be a completely different experience.

On the other hand, maybe that was a good thing. We weren't wrapped up in the complicated action on the ice. I'm not able to recall specific plays, but I am able to clearly recall the atmosphere and the sights and sounds of that night. My memory holds vivid impressions, not of the game, but of what it felt like to be in a crowd of 18,000 Kings fans.

I know that at the end of the first period, the score was 1-0 in favor of the Kings. One minute into the second period, the St. Louis Blues scored. Seconds later, Dwight King answered that goal, and the Kings were in the lead again.

The crowd never let up. I've been to a lot of concerts, but nothing compared to the way those fans rocked that building. I knew my ears would be ringing for days.

Halfway through the second period, Mike Richards scored. When the buzzer signaled the end of that period, the Kings were leading 3-1, and the fans were mildly hysterical.

I had hoped that I would be able to wear my wig throughout the game. But towards the end of the second period, my hot flashes kicked in.

Hot flashes are usually a curse for women going through menopause. They come on without warning. The sensation is like standing in front of a wood burning pizza oven with the door open. The wave of heat begins at your face and neck, which become bright red. The hot flash travels down your body, which causes you to sweat. The only way to find a little relief from the unbearable heat is to remove as much clothing as possible.

I stood up and removed my jacket, muffler and gloves.

The wig on my head had very little ventilation; my scalp felt hot enough to fry an egg on. Sweat started to stream down the sides of my face. I leaned over and whispered, "Cheryl, I really wanted to keep my wig on, but I'm starting to have hot flashes and the wig is making things worse. Do you mind if I take it off? If this is going to embarrass you, I completely understand. I'll just go to the restroom and air my head out for a few minutes."

Cheryl is one of the least pretentious people you will ever meet. She looked over at the hot mess I had become and didn't hesitate to exclaim, "Oh Melissa! Take off whatever you need to take off to make yourself comfortable! I don't give a hoot how you look!" Before she finished her sentence, I snatched that wig off and exposed my bald head to 18,000 fans.

When I stood up to stretch my legs, I glanced up into the stands. A few rows behind me, I spotted Matthew Perry staring at me-or my bald head. At first, I doubted my own eyes. Nah, that's not Matthew Perry, it's just somebody who strongly resembles him. I heard a nearby fan exclaim, "Oh look! There's Matthew Perry!" It really was Matthew Perry staring at me- or my bald head. A warm smile crossed his face and he nodded at me slightly. I waved to him and then sat down quickly before I did anything to embarrass myself.

With a two-goal lead, I felt confident that the Kings had it clinched. But four minutes into the third period, the Blues scored. The Kings were going to have to hold them back for sixteen minutes. Hockey minutes are like dog years. They seem to last much longer than normal minutes.

Unfolding before me was a brutal bloody, ballet. The Kings were battling with a grim determination. We were so close to the ice, I could see the toll that the intense play was taking on the team. Every player was drenched in sweat; their hair matted to their heads, rivulets of water running down the sides of their faces. They were constantly swiping at their foreheads in an effort to staunch the flow of sweat that was likely blurring their vision and stinging their eyes. Their breathing was labored; I watched their chests rise and fall rapidly, knowing that every intake of air must have been a burning in their lungs. Their faces, according to their complexion, were varying shades of red; flushed and agitated by overexertion. If there was the briefest pause in the game, the players would bend over at the waist, frantically sucking in air.

I closed my eyes for a few seconds. I could still feel the ebb and flow of the game by listening to the sounds of the crowd. There was a constant low buzz that would build with momentum until something exciting happened, then the fans would fill the arena with a deafening roar.

The tenacity and resolve of the Kings carried them from one play to another, and another. Instead of winding down as the game wore on, the team remained relentless and didn't give an inch.

The game was vicious, but the warrior spirit of each player was awe-inspiring. I began to wonder how it was possible for these players to keep fighting so fiercely, when clearly they were running on fumes. What was it that allowed them to remain engaged in this combat when physically they should have been dropping like flies?

The team had gone beyond the point of relying strictly on physical prowess and agility. The players had far surpassed depending upon their visceral strength, perfect passes, or exacting shots on goal. The part of their brain that was responsible for signaling their bodies to shut down had been overpowered by a savage drive to win. I was witness something truly rare; the power of the human spirit, that profound enigma that comes from deep within and empowers your body to do things it shouldn't be able to do. The Kings were willing themselves to keep on fighting. I realized that if I refused to give in to cancer, if I didn't give an inch, I would triumph over it.

Eight minutes into the fourth period, Drew Doughty scored. The final score of that game was 4-2.

During that unforgettable night, I went from being a Kings fan to being a Kings fanatic.

■■■

Three days later, the Kings faced the St. Louis Blues again. Game Four in the Western Conference Semifinals ended with a final score of LA Kings, 3, St. Louis Blues 1. The Kings had swept The Blues. This series marked the first time in NHL history that the eighth seed defeated both the first and second seeds.

One of the things I noticed as the playoffs progressed was how the Kings were able to communicate on the ice without using a single word. Sometimes it seemed as if they had eyes on the back of their heads. They were functioning as a single-minded, cohesive unit. Teamwork at it's finest.

The Conference Finals pitted the Kings against the Phoenix Coyotes. It was very nearly a second sweep; the end of this round brought the Kings into the Stanley Cup Finals with a 4-1 lead.

On May 30, the Stanley Cup Finals began. Our opposition was the New Jersey Devils. The first game of this series, an away game for The Kings, brought us closer to the cup. The score was tied 1-1 and went into sudden death overtime. Eight minutes into that period, Anze Kopitar scored the winning goal. The Kings were one game closer to realizing their dreams, and I only had one more chemotherapy session.

Game Two was a jubilant repetition of game one. Drew Doughty scored the first goal of the game in the first period, Ryan Carter of the Devils scored a goal in the third period. The game was tied and once again, we went into overtime. Thirteen minutes into overtime, Jeff Carter scored the winning goal for the Kings.

We were two wins away from the sweetest victory any team in the NHL will ever achieve. Every newspaper in the nation was covering the playoffs; every sports columnist agreed that this team had morphed from average to untouchable once they reached the playoffs. The Los Angeles Kings, the team that had been seeded eighth, had become the phoenix rising from the ashes.

Adding to the excitement during the playoffs was the breakout of a highly contagious disease known as Stanley Cup Fever. Kings fans were hanging huge banners from porches and business awnings. Small black flags touting the Kings logo were attached to car windows and could be seen snapping in the wind throughout Los Angeles streets and freeways. Front yards in every community posted signs of pride and encouragement, including mine. Kings fans didn't leave the house without sporting a Kings cap or t-shirt. Complete strangers would honk or wave, or share a high five while passing on the street. It didn't matter where you lived, how educated you were, what your annual salary or ethnic heritage was. Thousands of people, from every walk of life, became one tightly knit family. The fans wanted that cup in LA as badly as the team.

June 4, 2012, was a day of great celebration for two reasons. The

Kings beat the Devils 4-0 *and* I underwent my last chemotherapy treatment. I was wiped out that night, and I kept nodding off during the game. I would hear Michael suddenly scream out, which jolted me from my sleep. "Who scored?"

The answer was always, "The Kings!"

One more win stood between the Kings and the Stanley Cup Championship.

On June 6, 2012, I watched the game from behind our kitchen island. Our kitchen opens up into our den, which is where our large screen TV is located. I could not sit down during the game. I had to pace back and forth. Sometimes I would cover my eyes or ears, or leave the room entirely. The pressure was almost unbearable. I began to experience spikes in my blood pressure, which was weird because I have never had problems with high blood pressure.

Unfortunately, we did not win that game. The final score was 3-1.

The fifth game of the playoffs was an away game. As much as I wanted the Kings to capture that Cup, I wanted them to do it on home ice. The final score of that game was 2-1 in favor of the Devils. I knew my boys were coming home to claim their trophy.

Monday, June 11, 2012, brought the defining moment of glory to the Los Angeles Kings.

I watched the game from our sofa. I didn't need to cover my eyes or ears. My heart didn't race and my blood pressure didn't rise.

By the end of the first period, we were leading 3-0. Just a minute and a half into the second period, we scored again. At the very end of that period, the Devils scored, but with a 3-goal lead, I knew we had it locked up. I was actually feeling a little sorry for the Devils. It's one thing to lose a playoff game, but another thing to be pummeled into submission.

Sixteen minutes into the third period, Trevor Lewis scored his second goal of the game when the Devils left their net unattended. Fifteen seconds after that, Matt Greene scored another goal. The Stanley Cup was ours, yes, *ours*, with a final score of 6-1.

After a 45 year wait and a breathtaking playoff season, the Los Angeles Kings became the reigning champions of the NHL.

When the horn signaling the official end of the game sounded, black plastic streamers were released from the ceiling of The Staples Center, and fans began to toss hats onto the ice. The Kings rushed over to Jonathon Quick, forming a tight mass of black and white uniforms. Helmets and gloves and sticks were flying through the air. The players were clinging to each other and jumping up and down in joy.

Official presentations began with The Conn Smythe Trophy (Most Valuable Player During Playoff) being awarded Jonathon Quick.

The Stanley Cup was then presented to LA Kings captain Dustin Brown. He began the ritual of skating around the ice while hoisting the cup over his head and planting kisses on it. Each player was afforded the opportunity to take part in this ritual, to bask in the glow of this historical moment.

The intrepid spirit of this team had been my source of inspiration throughout chemotherapy. It also earned them a place in NHL history.

Once the Kings had taken possession of that magnificent silver cup, they very generously shared it with fans.

Just hours after the end of the championship game, the venerated trophy was the star attraction with patrons at a local Hermosa Beach pub. That night, team captain Dustin Brown had the privilege of being the first player to bring The Cup home.

On Tuesday evening, under a shower of glittery black and silver confetti, the Los Angeles Kings and Cup graced the stage of The Jimmy Kimmel Live Show. As soon as all the players were seated, Jimmy took a few steps back and remarked that the smell of beer was overpowering; apparently, the team was still celebrating.

On Wednesday, The Cup and the Kings celebrated at Dodger Stadium. Later that evening, Dustin Brown and The Cup made an appearance on the Tonight Show.

On Friday, some 250,00 people lined a one mile stretch of Figueroa Avenue in downtown Los Angeles. I was too weak to go to the parade, but fortunately it was televised, and I watched every minute. Players and their families rode atop various makeshift floats, waving enthusiastically to the raucous crowd. Confetti and streamers thrown from office building windows would flutter down and cover everyone beneath it.

The following Monday, a second parade took place. Thousands of fans lined a four-mile stretch between Redondo Beach and Manhattan Beach. I was still too weak to go out, but I was there in spirit.

HOT MOMMY

Moral of the Chapter: When You Are Going Through Hell,

Keep On Going

Winston Churchill

I was a different person after my battle with cancer. I learned to make the most of each and every day, to celebrate the small victories, to be grateful for the tiny joys and unaffected by the inconsequential annoyances of daily life. I was reveling in my recovery, but noticed that the fatigue from chemotherapy and radiation seemed to be lingering on.

I mentioned this to Dr. Angstreich at one of my monthly check up appointments. After running some blood work, he pointed out that my thyroid levels had been irregular since my first appointment with him. He suggested that I go to my general practitioner to follow up on that.

My general practitioner scheduled an ultrasound of my thyroid. The ultrasound indicated some areas of concern. I was referred to Kristen Egan, an ENT (Ear, Nose, Throat specialist). Dr. Egan was soft spoken and had a calmness about her. I immediately liked her. I was also impressed by the fact that she was eight months pregnant and wearing very high heels. What a trooper!

She performed a few tests and then made arrangements for me to have a needle biopsy done the following afternoon. I wasn't too worried about this thyroid thing. The possibility that I could be diagnosed with a second cancer never entered my mind. Also, the Kings were once again in the race for the Stanley Cup. I certainly didn't have time for a second cancer.

The day after the needle biopsy was performed, we met with Dr. Egan again.

The moment she opened the door into the exam room, it was obvious that the news was not good. The expression on her face said it all. She sat down on a wheeled stool and scooted over next to me until our knees were almost touching. Three words kept running through my mind. "This is bad, this is bad, this is bad." It was very bad.

On May 10, 2013, I was diagnosed with papillary thyroid cancer. After giving me this horrifying news, Dr. Egan immediately tried to calm us down by reassuring us that this cancer was nothing like breast cancer. Papillary thyroid cancer was what doctors referred to as "the good cancer," because it was easy to treat and beat. She began to explain the protocol for treating this diagnosis, explaining everything in a deliberate and comforting way.

My survival instincts began to run a ticker tape around my brain with the words: STAY CALM DO NOT PANIC STAY CALM DO NOT PANIC. I tried to focus on what Dr. Egan was saying, but the shock of hearing the "C" word made it nearly impossible to concentrate and pay attention to what we were being told. When I finally looked across the room at Michael, his face was grey. It was not white as a ghost, or white as a sheet; it was a sickly ashen gray. It resembled the color of my father's complexion right after he passed away in the hospital. My heart didn't begin to race until I saw the state that Michael was in; nothing was more petrifying than seeing his terror. He was my rock, my pillar of strength, my source of encouragement and comfort. If *he* fell apart, I was as good as dead.

"Honey, are you okay?"

Dr. Egan looked across the room, noted the color of Michael's skin, and asked him if he was going to faint. He was stoic when he said, "No." I wasn't sure if that meant no, he was not okay, or no, he was not going to faint. I began to try to reassure him by repeating the things that Dr. Egan had just told us. This was not like breast cancer; this was completely manageable by a simple surgery and medication for the rest of my life. I could not bring myself to repeat the phrase "This is the good cancer," but I kept up a steady stream of comparisons to reassure him that we could easily overcome this obstacle. Compared to breast cancer, this was a little hiccup. Within a few months, we would be able to continue on with our happily ever after.

Before we left her office, I told Dr. Egan that we had tickets to a Kings game for that night. I asked her if we could still go.

Michael's jaw dropped. "Are you kidding? You just found out that you have cancer! *Again*! How can you think about going to a King's game?"

I didn't want to start an argument in front of Dr. Egan so I ignored his question and waited for her reply. "Sure."

Once we were in the safety of our living room, Michael and I huddled on the sofa and clung to each other for dear life. When we were able to compose ourselves, I told Michael that all the blood had drained from his face when Dr. Egan said "the C word." I asked him what he had been feeling. He told me that he had felt betrayed by God. He had prayed so hard for these tests to reveal a benign tumor or cyst. He simply could not believe that God was going to allow me to face not only a second cancer, but a second cancer right on the heels of my first. He couldn't understand why this was happening to me.

I believed what Dr. Egan had told us, that this cancer was not going to be nearly as bad as breast cancer. I figured if I could beat breast cancer, I could beat thyroid cancer. I told Michael not to be angry with God. Whatever crisis was about to unfold, our only hope of weathering the storm was to rely upon our faith and trust. Without those as our anchor, we would be a tiny boat at the mercy of a howling nor' eastern squall.

At some point during our conversation, Michael asked if I was serious about going to the Kings game that night. I *was* serious. What better way to take my mind off our bad news? What else would give me a few hours of fun and positive energy? My survival instincts encouraged me to go to the source of my inspiration.

We went to watch the Kings vs. the St. Louis Blues. This was game number six of the quarterfinals. The final score was 2-1, in favor of the Kings. We were moving on to the semi-final run for the Stanley Cup. I enjoyed every minute of the game. I gloried in the enthusiasm of the fans. I did not think about thyroid cancer.

My connection to the team deepened. I am not a believer in mystical things like fortune tellers or tarot card readings. But here was a team that won the Stanley Cup for the first time in its forty-five year history at exactly the same time I was battling breast cancer. Now I had been diagnosed with thyroid cancer, and the team was once again embroiled in war to win The Cup. My inspiration was right there. The Kings and I were going to go into combat together again.

On May 23, the Kings would enter game number five of the semi-finals. The San Jose Sharks were their opponents; the series was tied 2-2. There is a fierce rivalry between the Kings and the Sharks, and this was a game that I did not want to miss.

Unfortunately, this was also the date of my thyroid surgery. It had become our practice for Michael to spend the night at the hospital after my surgeries but we had to make an exception this time. The hospital did not have cable channels or Wi-Fi. Since my surgery had gone smoothly and I had no adverse reaction to the anesthesia, I told Michael that he had to go home to watch the game. I made him promise to call me at the end of every period or whenever either team scored a goal. He kept his promise, but the following morning, I awoke with no recollection of our conversations. I called him in a panic to hear what the final score had been. The Kings had given the Sharks a royal beating--they had won the game 3-0!

I was released that morning but waited until we were home before looking into a mirror. There was not much to see because a thick gauze bandage had been wrapped around my throat many times. On the left side of my neck where the incision began, a drainage tube exactly like the ones I had after my breast surgery dangled down to my chest. A nurse had secured the bulb at the end of the tube by safety pinning it to the outside of my pajama top. This was not a pretty sight. The sight of the pink fluid dripping into the tubes made me woozy. I asked Michael to pin the bulb to the inside of my pajama top, so that its contents were not on display for any visitors I might receive. This was a good decision, because Eric and Emery came over to check on me that evening. My sons are the worst wusses when it comes to any ailments of the human body. They cannot stand the sight of blood, wounds, stitches, or anything that drains from your body. They praised me for my upbeat attitude and told me how proud they were that I was steadfast in being a brave little soldier. My sons are my heroes for many reasons; to receive their praise really cheered me up.

I went back to Dr. Egan's office the following week to have my drainage tube removed and my bandages changed. She said that I was healing nicely. I chose not to look when she removed the dressing. If possible, I like to see how I look after any surgery in the privacy of my own home. That way if I want to freak out, I can. Michael, of course, could not get close enough to inspect my new incision. He scrutinized the wound intensely, and then pronounced,

"Dr. Egan did a great job stitching you up! I don't think you're going to have much of a scar." Well, that was always good to hear.

The pain after the surgery had been minimal. The only problem I experienced was that I could not talk. Dr. Egan explained that during the surgery, my vocal chords had been stretched away from my thyroid. This caused a patient to temporarily lose their voice. The time it took to regain your voice was variable; it would be a subtle recovery that could take anywhere from a few weeks to a few months. I think Michael rather liked this side effect.

The Kings were putting up a tough fight against the San Jose Sharks. The semi-finals were brutal and lasted for seven games. In the end, the Kings were the winners.

The Stanley Cup Finals began on June 1, 2013. The opposing team was the Chicago Blackhawks, a formidable team full of outstanding players. The first two games were held in Chicago. I reverted back to my old ways of watching the game from our kitchen. The higher the stakes, the harder it was for me to keep my heart rate down.

We lost the first two games, but I felt certain that once the team returned to home ice, they would catch up.

I checked with Dr. Egan to make sure I was healthy enough to go to a game. She reminded me that my vocal chords were still recuperating, so it was important for me not to yell or scream during the game. My voice was hardly even a whisper then; even if I had wanted to, I would not have been able to scream or yell.

It had never been easy obtaining tickets to a playoff game, but it was much more challenging the year after the team won the Stanley Cup. Michael and I had to settle for seats in the 300 section, which was the section farthest from the ice. To our surprise, the seats gave us an awesome vantage point of the game. It was much easier to see the strategy of the team from this distance and for some reason, easier to follow the puck.

Three minutes into the first period, Justin Williams scored the first goal of the game. During one of my online researches about hockey, I read that statistically speaking, the first team that scores has a 67% chance of winning the game. Fans go crazy when their team scores first.

Six minutes into the second period, Slava Voynov scored a second goal. I was swept up with the enthusiasm of the crowd, and temporarily forgot that I was not supposed to use my voice. I jumped to my feet and let out a whoop-but what filled the air around me sounded nothing like a whoop. It sounded like Chewbacca had shown up to the game! My section fell silent; anyone within earshot stopped cheering and began looking around for the source of that primal groan. A muffler was wrapped around my neck, but the white gauze dressing was peeking over the top of the scarf. I could feel the stares coming from every direction. I stood frozen in front of my seat for a few seconds. I pulled the scarf from around my neck to reveal the thick white bandages and shrugged my shoulders as if to say, "Sorry."

I hadn't known what the reaction would be but I sure didn't expect the resounding outburst of applause and cheers. This is a great example of what LA Kings fans are like. I was so touched by this show of compassion and support, my eyes welled up with tears. I wrapped my scarf back around my neck and sat down. There's no better medicine than a hockey game.

Forty seconds before the end of the second period, the Blackhawks scored their first goal.

Thirty seconds before the end of the third period, Dwight King scored a goal. I didn't make a peep. We had our first win against the Blackhawks and it was sweet.

Two nights later, the teams battled it out again. Even though we were on home ice, the Kings were defeated by one goal.

Both teams fought like champions during the final game of the playoffs. I stood in our kitchen but faced away from the television screen. Mostly, I just listened to the game. When it went into overtime, I took a mild tranquilizer. That turned out to be a very smart decision, because at the end of the first overtime, the teams were still tied. Sadly, during the second overtime, the Blackhawks scored first and the final score was 4-3.

The run for the Stanley Cup ended here for the Kings but what a run it had been. This phenomenal team had once again inspired me throughout a battle with cancer. "My boys" didn't let me down.

Thyroid cancer was not the walk in the park that I believed it would be. There were a plethora of side effects that lingered for months. The most obvious was my voice. For the first few months after surgery, it was breathy and soft, like Jackie Onassis' voice. When I finally developed some tone, what came out of my mouth was a man's voice. Not just a man's voice, a very deep man's voice. This was a constant source of embarrassment. Sometimes when I answered the phone, my own family would say, "Hi Michael!"

We took a brief vacation to San Francisco during my recovery; this was the first time I noticed that when Michael and I went to a restaurant, patrons sitting at nearby tables would stare at me. When I went to see Dr. Egan for a check up, she said it was probably taking longer for my voice to return to normal because I had already been in a weakened condition before I had the thyroid surgery. My body wasn't bouncing back as quickly because of the beating it had taken during breast cancer. She suggested that I go to a speech therapist, but I resisted. I was just so sick of doctor appointments.

In early August, I continued on to the second step in my treatment for thyroid cancer. This consisted of having RAI or Iodine-131 therapy, which takes the prize for the most bizarre medical procedure I've ever had. The process was so complicated I have to break it down into four parts in order to explain it.

The purpose of having the RAI-131 therapy is to destroy any cancer cells that may have survived after surgery. In order for the test to be most effective, a patient has to have high levels of thyroid stimulating hormone (TSH) in his or her blood. This hormone stimulates thyroid tissue and cancer cells, which absorb the radioactive iodine. Once you have had your thyroid removed, you are immediately placed on a synthetic Thyroid hormone. So Part One required me to quit taking my medication for two weeks.

You would think that having your TSH level rise would cause you to become hyperactive, but the opposite of that is true. A high TSH level makes you dog tired, depressed, and unable to concentrate. I was dreading this part of the test. There is a shortcut that avoids having to suffer through these weeks of misery. An injection known as Thyrotropin or Thyrogen can be given to the patient; this medication stimulates the TSH immediately. The patient is able to ingest the radioactive iodine with the CAT scan following immediately. Patients who are currently taking any anti-depressant medications are encouraged to skip the pain period and go right to the Thyrotropin injection because severe depression can be a side effect of a high TSH.

Neither Michael nor I can remember why I did not just take that injection. It wasn't like I was some bad ass that didn't want to tap out: I was physically and emotionally drained at that time. The only reason I can imagine not taking that injection was perhaps because it was not covered by our insurance, but even that seems unlikely. We had already shelled out thousands of dollars in medical expenses. I strongly encourage any readers who are dealing with thyroid cancer to avoid that abysmal period and get the shot.

Part two of the thyroid therapy involved following a strict diet that prohibited the patient from eating any foods that contain iodine, Red Dye #3, dairy products, eggs, seafood, or soy sauce.

The Red Dye #3 was easy, as were soy sauce, seafood, and eggs. The dairy products were more of a struggle for me because I love cheese and yogurt, but I knew I could do without for two or three weeks. Finding foods that were iodine free was ridiculously difficult. Any food that has salt in it has iodine in it. Once I began thoroughly inspecting food labels, I was shocked to see how many foods contained salt as an additive. After my breast cancer, I cut sugar and processed foods out of my diet by about 90%. My blood tests improved drastically, but I only lost about five pounds. (I didn't know it at the time, but thyroid cancer was messing with my metabolism.)

The sugar free, salt free, dairy free diet really sucked. But I did it.

At the end of those two very long weeks, I went to the hospital to have blood drawn. Before I could ingest the radioactive iodine, my TSH level had to be at a specific level. The endocrinologist called me later that afternoon to tell me that my blood level was not high enough to go forward with the test. She advised me that it was necessary for me to remain on the diet for one more week. By then, it wasn't the diet that was pushing me over the edge; it was the miserable fatigue and depression that was reminiscent of life during chemo. I whimpered when I heard that I had to suffer through another whole week; I told the endocrinologist that one more week was my limit. If my level wasn't high enough by then, I wanted the injection.

Fortunately, when I went back for my second blood test, my TSH level was high enough to go forward with ingesting the radioactive iodine.

Part three of the therapy consisted of going to the hospital to ingest the radioactive iodine. I was terrified about having to ingest that radioactive iodine. During the period of time that my body was elevating my TSH, I started having panic attacks. If I began to dwell on taking that radioactive iodine, a panic attack would strike.

I had watched the movie *Silkwood* many times. This is the true story of Karen Silkwood, a metallurgist at a plutonium factory who was purposefully contaminated because she was going to expose worker safety violations at the plant in which she worked. The movie contained harrowing scenes of what happened to employees who had been exposed to plutonium. This included having to stand in a scalding hot shower while having every inch of their body scrubbed raw. The movie also revealed what was happening to employees who had been continually exposed to plutonium. There were a shockingly high number of cancer victims. The type of cancer was not limited to one; employees presented with a wide spectrum of cancers. One scene in particular had really stayed with me; it was of a middle-aged, nearly bald woman who had developed cancer but thought she was in remission. She had just undergone some kind of test that indicated her hair was growing back "hot." (Radioactive.) I could not get the morbid mental images of *Silkwood* out of my head.

Michael came home a little early one evening to find me sitting on the steps in our back yard; my head was cradled in my arms and I was sobbing.

He sat down and put his arm around my shoulders. "Honey, what's the matter?"

"I'm terrified to take that radioactive pill!"

"Of course you are. Nobody wants to be radioactive! But this is all done under very specific guidelines. They've done plenty of research. You're just going to have to drink a shitload of water to get the RAI out of your system. Once it's out, it's gone forever."

"Well, but look at the horrible things that happened to the people in

Silkwood! That one lady who was bald found out that her hair was growing back in hot! What if this stuff goes to my scalp and I have to shave my head again!"

He thought about that for a second, and then pulled away from me to ask, "What medications did you take today?"

"What? What medications did I take? I took what I usually take."

"You didn't double down on anything? You didn't skip anything?"

"No. Why?"

"Because you're not making sense. You're talking about *Silkwood*, the movie about Karen Silkwood, right?"

"Right."

"Karen Silkwood worked in a *plutonium* factory. You're not taking plutonium. You're not going to be anywhere near plutonium. You are taking radioactive iodine. The two elements are worlds apart." I felt much better after that.

The fourth part to this therapy begins by going into the bowels of the hospital where the nuclear medicine department is located. This is a scary place. There are hazard signs posted *everywhere*. I kept waiting to see signs with a skull and crossbones. Once you are placed in an exam room, the process moves with a frightening speed. I felt like everyone I came into contact with was treating me like I was a carrier of the Ebola Virus. A nurse wearing a lead apron zipped into the exam room. She was using a long set of tongs to hold a tiny white cup in front of her. Right away, your survival instincts want to know: Why is she using tongs to hold the cup that holds the medicine I am about to swallow? The answer is, that tiny pill encapsulates one hundred millicuries of radioactive iodine, some of which leak into the air around it. I think the nurse's goal is to get in and out of that room as quickly as humanly possible. She holds the tongs that hold that cup that holds the pill out to you and stands back. She watches you swallow it. She races out of the room.

Michael had rooted around in his laboratory at work and found a radiation counter. He stuck it in his briefcase and smuggled it home. I should have seen that coming. He brought it to the hospital; this elicited a very hostile reaction from the radiologist. She practically recoiled when he showed it to her. She insisted that he put it away because it was unnecessary and imprudent for him to use it on me. We totally ignored her opinion.

These were the aftercare instructions I was given before I left the hospital:

> Sit as far away from the driver as you can on your drive home from the hospital.
>
> Sequester yourself into one room of your home.
>
> Do not come into contact with any other living being for three days.
>
> Put on disposable gloves before you touch anything.
>
> Use paper plates and glasses, and plastic cutlery. When disposing of them, make sure they are sealed in a plastic bag before placing them in your regular trash receptacle.
>
> Wash the clothes that you wore to the hospital separately from other laundry. (I threw mine away. Seriously.)
>
> Wash anything you wear or touch separately from other laundry. (Clothes, sheets, towels, etc.)
>
> You cannot share a bathroom. Your body eliminates the radioactive iodine through your urine. You have

to flush twice after every pee, because your urine is "hot."

We had decided that I would stay in my studio while I was radioactive. My studio is a very small room located off our kitchen. It contains all of my crafting supplies. We purchased a twin sized bed and squeezed it into the room. Off the hallway that connects our laundry room to our kitchen is a very tiny bathroom that consists simply of a toilet and a sink. I didn't want to close the French doors that separated the studio from the kitchen because the space already felt like a prison cell. We had to create some kind of a barrier between the two rooms to prevent the dog and the cats from joining me. Our solution was a baby gate. I was expecting to spend two or three days in that room. Two or three days didn't seem like such a long time.

I ingested my radioactive pill and was immediately escorted through a labyrinth of corridors that led to the hospital parking lot. Michael couldn't wait to break out that Geiger counter. I had planned on riding in the back seat of our SUV, but when Michael looked at the reading on the Geiger counter, he asked me if I would mind laying down in the cargo area of the car. Obviously, he was trying to maximize the distance between the two of us. Even more alarming was the speed at which we flew home. Michael, who usually drives like Miss Daisy, had turned into Mario Andretti. He was definitely freaked out by my numbers.

As soon as we arrived home, I began to drink quart after quart of water. The first time I peed, Michael could not resist scanning the toilet seat. This was a scene right out of *Silkwood*. When the meter began to squelch rapidly and loudly, he quickly backed out of the bathroom. I was drinking so much water I could hear it slosh around in my belly, but my radioactive level was inching down in miniscule increments. Every hour, Michael would stand about four feet away from me and point the Geiger counter toward my body. He didn't seem too concerned that the level was dropping so slowly. I didn't get much sleep that night, but every time I peed, I knew I was getting rid of some radioactivity.

By day number four, my levels were still far too high for me to re-enter the world. The studio was feeling smaller by the hour. The hardest thing to deal with was our dog, Random Task. He would sit (sit, not lay) on the other side of the baby gate for hours, begging me with his velvety brown eyes to let him in. I love this dog with all my heart; we spend all day every day together. He didn't understand why I refused to let him in, and it broke my heart to have to ignore him. I heard Michael trying to explain the situation to him one evening.

"Random, you can't be near Mommy right now. Mommy is hot. If you stand next to her, you'll be a hot dog." Even in my miserable state, I had to laugh.

Day five, I busted out of my cell. My radioactive levels should have been much lower but I threatened Michael that if I had to stay in that room for one more day, I was going to get a huge tattoo, like prisoners get. I wore disposable gloves for a few more days, I continued to use the tiny bathroom, and Michael and I kept a three foot distance between the two of us.

I once read that if a human being is deprived of contact from other human beings for an extended period of time, they become deranged. I now have a deep appreciation for that theory.

One week after ingesting the RAI, I went back to the nuclear medicine department in the hospital to have a body scan. By far, this was the easiest part of the ordeal. I was placed on a table that moved my body very slowly through a machine that was shaped like a donut. Inch by inch, my body was x-rayed as I passed through the hole of the donut.

I don't remember what I was told after that test. Everything must have been fine because I was released and never had to return for a repeat test.

I began the exhaustive process of finding a good endocrinologist who would address the awful symptoms that besieged me after my thyroid was removed. I switched physicians three times before I had to admit to myself that as long as your thyroid levels are good, your endocrinologist thinks their job is done. The problem with that is, your thyroid level might be clinically fine, but you can still feel like dog shit. Breast cancer only affects your breasts-but your thyroid is in charge of many systems in your body.

My physical symptoms include eyebrows that randomly fall, and leg cramps that are so painful they make me scream. No matter what the weather is, I am always hot. No matter how much sleep I get, I am always tired. A trip to the grocery store is exhausting to me. I'm always dizzy and can't walk down a flight of stairs without holding onto the railing.

My mental acuity is shot and my brain always feels clouded.

At least once a day, every day, Michael hears these questions:

"Have you seen my (reading/distance) glasses?"

"Have you seen my car keys?"

"Have you seen my purse?"

I lost two pairs of expensive sunglasses, a hearing aid, and the diamond earrings that Michael bought me for our tenth anniversary.

I used to have a great sense of direction. I get lost all the time now, even though my car has a GPS system. I've driven out to my sister's house in Orange County hundreds of times. The last time I drove out there, I completely zoned out on the drive home and somehow ended up in Whittier, which is about 45 minutes in the wrong direction.

I've taken my 4Runner to the body shop way too many times this year. I seem to have developed a depth perception problem. I'm constantly jumping curbs, which is always embarrassing. There is a ridiculously tight turn out of the parking lot in my optometrist's office; if you don't gauge it exactly right, you are pitted against a tall cement wall. I always take that turn very slowly, and up until a month ago, I've been successful in executing the turn. On my last visit to the doc, I didn't judge the turn correctly, and that resulted in a series of deep gashes to the passenger side of my car. If I'm driving down a narrow street and there is a car in the oncoming lane, I seem to over-compensate by veering too far to the right. If there happens to be a parked SUV with a large side-view mirror sticking out, I knock it off with my huge right side-view mirror that is sticking out. You would be amazed at what a loud sound that makes. There have been many occasions when I've had to call Michael (he's in the house) on my cell phone (I am in my car) to say, "Honey, I was backing out of the driveway and I knocked all of our trash cans over. Our garbage is spewing down the street."

My 95 year old mother can beat me at most board games.

I have twice accidentally taken Random Task's medication, and twice accidentally given him mine. For the safety and well being of my beautiful baby, I've abdicated the dispensing of Random's medications to Michael.

I used to be quick with a quip, but now I struggle to remember the most common words, like seatbelt or squirrel. There was a time when I knew far more about the game of hockey than Michael-but I've forgotten so much that now he is more knowledgeable about the game.

This condition is frustrating for both Michael and me. I get flustered and angry for doing stupid things all the time. Michael tries really hard to remain patient with me, but when I do a series of lame things in a short period of time, he becomes aggravated-which only makes the situation worse. If you're living with someone whose mental clarity has been impaired by any cancer, try to remember that this condition makes the victim of this curse feel dim witted and powerless. Pointing out their shortcomings only makes it worse.

I am eight years into my recovery from thyroid cancer. I have yet to find an endocrinologist who will do more than look at my blood test results and tell me my thyroid levels are fine. I still have bouts of hair loss, my fatigue is ever-present, getting a good night's sleep is a rarity, and hot flashes are a part of my life. I have problems with concentration and am hopelessly forgetful. My levels may be fine, but *I* am not fine. I pray for the day when I'm restored to a normal, healthy person.

HAT TRICK

Moral of the Chapter: That which does not kill us, makes us stronger

Friedrich Nietzsche

In late September 2013, I noticed a tiny, very dark freckle on the front of my right calf. Most people would have probably ignored this little spot, but I had reason to be concerned.

In 2001, my dermatologist had done a scraping very near the vicinity of this freckle. The biopsy revealed basal cell carcinoma. The dermatologist went back in and removed a large, deep swath of tissue. Fortunately, the margins had been wide and clean and there had been no reason to believe the cancer would return. The stitches that had been placed both inside and outside the wound had ruptured before the area healed, leaving me with a really ugly two-inch scar and a patch of badly discolored skin on my leg.

Since that incident I had been ever vigilant about checking my body for any weird spots.

Upon finding that little black spot, I hightailed it to a dermatologist. I showed her the spot I was concerned about; when she inspected my leg, she pointed out two other areas that she thought were "highly suspicious." She asked to see my left calf, where she found two more "highly suspicious" areas.

These areas had not resembled anything that looked cancerous to me, but apparently I didn't know what cancerous looked like.

I didn't ask any questions. I didn't want to hear about the various types of skin cancer. I didn't want to know the statistics. I didn't want to educate myself. I refused to believe that I had one more damn cancer cell in my body.

One week before the opening game of the 2013-14 hockey season, my dermatologist performed five skin scrapes; three on my right calf, two on my left calf. I don't know why they are called scrapes. Your skin is not scraped; it is scooped. The doctor digs out a scoop much larger and deeper than the actual area of concern, ensuring clean margins just in case the pathology report indicates any type of cancer. My calves were first numbed by injections of anesthetics and then deep divots were dug out of my flesh. I left the office with bandages wrapped around both legs. Beneath those bandages were twenty-eight stitches. When the anesthetic wore off, the pain was excruciating. Thank God my medicine cabinet contained some painkillers that were leftover from my two previous cancers.

Three days later, I returned to the dermatologist's office. She handed me a copy of the pathology report, and gave me a minute to look it over. It contained five different diagnosis'; one for each chunk of skin that had been scooped out of my calves. I did not see the word malignant or carcinoma anywhere on the page. As far as I could tell, I was in the clear.

The doctor cleared her throat and began by saying that we could rule four of the five biopsies non-malignant. She then leaned over and circled the section marked "D" on the report I was holding. *Lentiginous junctional nevus.* Her voice was very grave. "This one has me very concerned. This could be a serious problem."

No. No. No. I wanted to cover my ears and do that thing that kids do when they don't want to hear what is being said to them. I wanted to smack the doctor. I was not afraid: I was furious.

I glared at the doctor and waited.

"This diagnosis is often a precursor to melanoma. Statistically, patients with this condition have a 64% chance of this area turning cancerous. With your medical history that statistic could be even higher. This is bad."

I experienced a fleeting moment of déjà vu when she spoke those last three words. To prevent myself from freaking out, I focused on the word "precursor." To me, precursor translated to "Let's cross that bridge when we come to it." I beat breast cancer and thyroid cancer. I knew that if this *lentiginous* stuff morphed into melanoma, I would kick its ass, too.

Three cancer diagnoses in three consecutive years. When I think of things that come in three, I think of hat tricks. Ha. This was my cancer hat trick!

Four days later, I cautiously and slowly walked through the Staples Center and down the steps that led to our seats. It was the first home game of the season for the LA Kings, and no amount of stitches could have prevented me from being there. I had attended games in far worse condition.

I glanced around the arena where thousands had gathered. I knew that a high percentage of those surrounding me had one problem or another. Some of these people had financial worries, some hated their job, some were stuck in an unhappy relationship, and some had a kid who was battling drug addiction. How many wigs hid heads that were bald due to chemotherapy? Nobody gets through this life without a certain amount of suffering. The remarkable and wonderful thing was, all the fans were able to check their troubles at the door. For about three hours, we would scream and cheer and laugh, we would celebrate every goal and stunning play our team executed. Or, we might be angry or disappointed or even a little disgusted. What we would not be doing is dwelling on our problems.

We were given about three worry free hours, courtesy of The Los Angeles Kings.

The lights were dimmed and the Jumbotron began playing the opening video. I smiled and sat back in my seat. A new season was here, and I was cancer free.

The Los Angeles Kings were the 2013-14 Stanley Cup Champions.

Fifteen seconds of fame on the Jumbotron

To read more stories, see pictures of me with the Kings, ask questions, or just give me a shout out, please visit me at:

www.melissashattrick.com

I would love to hear from you!